Y0-BSQ-351

An Evangelical Agenda

1984 and beyond

An Evangelical Agenda

1984 and beyond

Addresses, Responses,
and Scenarios from the
"Continuing Consultation on
Future Evangelical Concerns"
held in Overland Park, Kansas,
December 11-14, 1979.

Sponsored by the Billy Graham Center
Wheaton College

William Carey Library

1705 N. SIERRA BONITA AVE. • PASADENA, CALIFORNIA 91104

Library of Congress Cataloging in Publication Data

Continuing Consultation on Future Evangelical Concerns,
    Overland Park, Kan., 1978.
    An evangelical agenda, 1984 and beyond.

    1. Evangelicalism--United States--Congresses.
2. Forecasting--Congresses. I. Billy Graham Center.
II. Title.
BR1642.U5C67 1978   230   79-15889
ISBN 0-87808-171-2

Copyright © 1979 by The Billy Graham Center

All rights reserved.

No part of this book may be used or reproduced in any manner whatsoever without written permission, except in the
case of brief quotations embodied in critical articles and re-
views.

Published by the William Carey Library
1705 N. Sierra Bonita Avenue
Pasadena, California 91104
Telephone (213) 798-0819

In accord with some of the most recent thinking of the academic press, the William Carey Library is pleased to present
this scholarly book which has been prepared from an author-
edited and author-prepared camera ready copy.

PRINTED IN THE UNITED STATES OF AMERICA

30.0631
767e

L.I.F.E. College Library
1100 Glendale Blvd.
Los Angeles, Calif. 90026

LIFE Pacific College
Alumni Library
1100 West Covina Blvd.
San Dimas, CA 91773

Contents

025656

PART III -- SCENARIOS

Foreword

Our age is characterized by increasing uncertainty about
the future and by mounting anxieties that are both personal
and corporate. The questions of survival in the event of a
nuclear holocaust are being asked with even greater frequency
than they were in 1945. New concerns have arisen to challenge this chronic one as the world faces the possibility
of such things as a massive energy shortage, a world-wide
monetary crisis resulting from runaway inflation, or an
overpopulated planet. For the Christian there is the prospect of moral and ethical disintegration in the society in
which he lives and the distinct possibility of rejection
or even persecution in a world increasingly hostile to the
Gospel.

The Consultation described in this volume attempted to
develop a perspective that was realistic rather than naively
optimistic or hopelessly pessimistic. A sense of urgency
and a sense of trust were both evident in the general sessions and in private conversations.

The results of the Consultation have yet to be fully
assessed. Certainly there was a greater appreciation of
the situation in our world today. Christian leaders enlarged the circle of friendship and developed a greater respect and understanding of one another's viewpoints. But
the real test of the effectiveness of this Consultation lies
in what difference it will make within the Christian community in the days to come.

That is one of the major reasons for this book. We believe that what was presented at the Consultation deserves the attention and the response of the entire evangelical community. We trust also that it will be the basis for conferences in the future that will continue to enlarge the vision of God's people and enable them to have a still more effective stewardship of time and opportunity in these critical days.

Hudson T. Armerding
Chairman

Preface

Having accepted the additional responsibilities of "Acting Director" of the Billy Graham Center at Wheaton College during the intervening year between the 1977 and 1978 Consultations, I attended the "Continuing Consultation on Future Evangelical Concerns" as one of the nineteen "first timers" who had not participated in the 1977 Consultation.

I was thrilled with the new vistas which opened before my eyes. I returned from the conference with a deep awareness of a need for flexibility in the form and methodology of the church, for my responsibility to my own family, for the deep human needs of a secular society crying out for response from the church, and for the absolute imperative to bring the Gospel to the unreached peoples of the world.

Another first-time participant, Dr. Harry Evans, president of Trinity College, was quoted in the college's publication, *Trinity Today*, as saying:

> The overwhelming consensus [of the participants in the Consultation] was that the stance of the faithful, biblical Christian church will be more and more in conflict with society in regard to marriage, sexuality, family stability, lifestyle, and other values. There is white water ahead for the church. This conference was clearly the very best I have ever attended.

Dr. Evans' feelings, I'm sure, were shared by all of the participants.

This publication consists of the addresses, responses, and group scenarios presented at the Consultation held in Overland Park, Kansas, December 11 to 14, 1978. The 1978 Consultation was the continuation of the earlier "Consultation on Future Evangelical Concerns," held in Atlanta, Georgia, in December, 1977, The first one grew out of an *ad hoc* meeting of twenty-three evangelical leaders in March, 1977, called to consider the future of the church and evangelicalism during the remainder of the Twentieth Century. Under the sponsorship of the Billy Graham Center at Wheaton College, eighty participants met in Atlanta to focus on the future. The book, *Evangelicals Face the Future*, edited by Donald E. Hoke and published by William Carey Library for the Billy Graham Center, contains the proceedings of the 1977 Consultation.

These papers, then, comprise the second volume -- or Part II, so to speak -- of the earlier publication. Where the 1977 Consultation dealt with the future through the end of this century, the 1978 Consultation dealt with the *intermediate* future, "1984 and Beyond."

This Consultation was chaired by Dr. Hudson T. Armerding, president of Wheaton College, and the planning and coordination was the responsibility of Dr. Donald E. Hoke -- both men repeating the roles they filled in 1977. They were ably assisted by a planning committee, also chaired by Dr. Armerding, composed of: Drs. John W. Alexander, Leighton Ford, Herschel H. Hobbs, Kenneth S. Kantzer, and Ted Ward. Dr. Tom Sine performed the very key role of facilitating the "breakout" study groups as they worked to write the scenarios presented in Part III of this volume.

Each day's program began with a period of worship, highlighted by a Bible study series presented by Dr. Edmund P. Clowney, focusing on the church as a pilgrim people and a missionary assembly.

Following Coordinator Hoke's perceptive conference overview, Dr. Leighton Ford's keynote address challenged the participants with the urgency of the Consultation goal as evidenced by its theme, through a vivid, contemporary recounting of Noah's mission in the needy world of his time.

Preceded by major presentations of the utopian and dystopian perspectives on the future by eminently qualified futurists, "An Evangelical Agenda -- 1984 and Beyond" dealt with "The Future of the Church" in four major aspects: Nurture,

Form, and Function; The Christian Family; In a Secular Society; and World Evangelization.

As in the 1977 Consultation, the format was designed to combine the advantages of small study groups and large plenary sessions. Each major paper's presentation to a plenary session was followed by a brief response from a Consultation participant selected in advance. Opportunity had been afforded participants beforehand for input to the speakers; some of the addresses refer to these specific areas of emphases and interest. Since, contrary to the 1977 format, responders had been instructed to *summarize* and *capsulize* the assigned paper rather than *debate the issues* raised, it should be noted that the response following each address focuses attention on the issues raised in that paper and does not necessarily represent the viewpoint of the respondent; some responders, however, you will find, do make additions, call attention to omissions, or urge cautions.

Following the plenary sessions' major address and formal response and before breaking into the in-depth study group sessions, a period was scheduled for questions and comments from the entire group.

The scenarios represent the culminating "products" of the study groups; they vary in thrust and emphasis, reflecting, of course, the membership of that particular group and the expertise of the "scribe."

Following the scenarios' presentation at the concluding morning session, the Consultation participants engaged in a warm time of fellowship, sharing, and prayer. This time of fellowship and prayer was marked by a deep sense of appreciation for the unity of the church and the commitment of all the participants -- represented by a wide range of constituencies -- to the one true Gospel. This time of expression of deep appreciation, one for another, is one I shall not soon forget.

An entire record of the proceedings at the Consultation is available on cassette tapes. These may be obtained by writing to: The Billy Graham Center, P. O. Box 674, Wheaton, Illinois 60187. These tapes are available because of the very significant contribution made by Mr. Harry Dickelman who participated in the Consultation and handled all the audio and visual arrangements.

All of the participants in the Consultation join me in an expression of deep appreciation to Mrs. Jane Nelson of the Billy Graham Center staff. Mrs. Nelson handled the logistical arrangements for the Consultation from the beginning of the planning through the Consultation itself. She is responsible also for the editing and preparation for final printing of all the materials in this volume.

I must also express to the TWA Breech Training Academy the appreciation of all the participants for the excellent facilities and service over and beyond that which was required.

It is our hope that as you share the work of the Consultation by reading this volume, you will gain some sense of the issues facing the church in our modern secular society.

David E. Johnston
Director, Billy Graham Center

Program Personnel

HUDSON T. ARMERDING -- Fifth president of Wheaton College; president, World Evangelical Fellowship; and past president, National Association of Evangelicals.

WILLIAM C. BROWNSON, JR. -- Radio and television minister, "Words of Hope," Reformed Church in America.

LEIGHTON FORD -- Associate evangelist and vice president, Billy Graham Evangelistic Association; popular speaker, author, and articulate voice for world evangelization, he is serving his second term as chairman, Lausanne Committee for World Evangelization.

WILLIAM H. GARRISON -- Prominent Dallas attorney and active layman, he is vice chairman of the Dallas Theological Seminary board.

GENE A. GETZ -- Currently pastor, Fellowship Bible Church, Dallas, and Adjunct Professor of Pastoral Ministries, Dallas Theological Seminary.

WILLIS W. HARMAN -- Author, government consultant, and lecturer -- a leading futurist spokesman -- now associate director, Center for the Study of Social Policy, Urban and Social Systems Division, Stanford Research Institute.

HOWARD G. HENDRICKS -- Professor of Christian Education, Dallas Theological Seminary, he is a popular author and lecturer -- in demand for family life seminars and conferences.

PETER J. HENRIOT -- Author, lecturer, and teacher at numerous
North American universities, including MIT-Harvard's Center
for Urban Studies and Seattle University, he is currently
director, Center of Concern, Washington, D.C.; he has worked
in Latin America and participated in UN-sponsored population
conferences in the U.S. and Europe.

DONALD E. HOKE -- Presently pastor, Cedar Springs Presbyterian Church, Knoxville, Tennessee, he has been a theological
educator in the U.S. and Japan. Following the directorship
of the 1974 International Congress on World Evangelization,
Lausanne, Switzerland, he served as the Billy Graham Center's
first executive director.

DAVID E. JOHNSTON -- Vice president for finance, Wheaton College, and director, Billy Graham Center, following the executive vice presidency, Trinity College.

RICHARD F. LOVELACE -- Noted authority and writer in the
field of church history, he is Professor of Church History,
Gordon-Conwell Theological Seminary.

GORDON MAC DONALD -- Senior pastor, Grace Chapel, Lexington,
Massachusetts, and lecturer on practical theology at Gordon-
Conwell, Covenant, and Conservative Baptist Theological
Seminaries.

J. ROBERTSON MC QUILKIN -- Former missionary to Japan, he is
president, Columbia Bible College and Graduate School of
Bible and Missions.

ARMAND M. NICHOLI, JR., M.D. -- Faculty member, Harvard Medical School, and staff member, Massachusetts General Hospital,
he also maintains a private practice of psychiatry; visiting
lecturer at universities in the U.S. and abroad, he is editor
and principal author of the widely used and highly praised
The Harvard Guide to Modern Psychiatry; his research has
focused on teens, young adults, and family problems.

JOHN M. PERKINS -- Evangelical leader, speaker, and author,
he is president and founder of Voice of Calvary Ministries,
headquartered in Jackson, Mississippi.

LARRY W. POLAND -- Former president, Miami Christian College,
he is director of the Agape Movement, Campus Crusade for
Christ, International.

CATHY STONEHOUSE -- Director of curriculum ministries, Light & Life Press, Free Methodist Publishing House, Winona Lake, Indiana.

TED WARD -- Director, Michigan State University's Values Development Education Program, he is Professor of Curriculum Research, assigned to the Institute for International Studies; also serves as consultant to universities, government agencies, and evangelical mission organizations.

RALPH D. WINTER -- Founder and director, U.S. Center for World Mission, his career as educator, author, missionary, and missiologist has earned him the reputation of being one of today's most creative influences for world evangelization, focusing his ministry on the world's unreached peoples.

PART I

Overview and Keynote Address

Introduction

Donald E. Hoke

May I add my word of cordial welcome to that of President Armerding. For those of you who are here for the first time, this second "Consultation on Future Evangelical Concerns" will follow the goals and patterns of the first held last December. The response to that was so enthusiastic that the participants felt this second conference would be profitable both for them and for an additional number of invited guests. May I then restate the goals and guidelines for this year's Consultation:

1. To raise our consciousness concerning the problems of future change and to enable us to become more abreast of breathtaking advances in areas of knowledge outside of, but impinging on, our own specialities.

2. To focus our attention more specifically this year on the future of Christ's church. How will it be affected and how should it respond? Change is the one absolute of modern society. Exponential growth in knowledge, science, and technology are the change makers. Creative adaptability and response must be the evangelical agenda for 1984 and beyond.

3. To inject a note of urgency -- as reflected by our theme -- I conclude to be my particular role tonight.

Perhaps I can best establish this mood of urgency by updating some pages from George Orwell's best-selling book of

1949 that gave us the peg on which to hang this year's theme,
"An Evangelical Agenda -- 1984 and Beyond!" I'm quoting extensively from an article in the December 1978 issue of *The
Futurist* magazine by Dr. David Goodman, manager of a consult-
ing group of scientists (many psychobiologists, like himself)
that deals with the future and the human brain.

George Orwell wrote *1984* to warn the Western world
about what he thought the future might hold. But
though Orwell succeeded in creating a gripping vision
of a thought-controlled totalitarian world, his novel
has failed to halt the forces that he saw leading the
way towards totalitarianism. Now with only a few
years to go until 1984, the Western world is potentially much closer to his vision than most people realize. Though *1984* has failed as a warning, it has
been succeeding brilliantly as a forecast.

In the novel *1984*, Orwell pictures a world controlled
by three great superpowers -- Oceania, Eurasia, and
Eastasia -- which wage continuous warfare of limited
arms in a quadrilateral of land that includes much of
Africa, the Middle East, and Southeast Asia. Today,
the U.S., the U.S.S.R., and China struggle to gain
influence throughout the Third World.

Goodman and his associates identified 137 specific predictions Orwell made in *1984*. They were divided into two cat-
gories

    -- Scientific and technological

    -- Social and political

In 1972 he found that eighty had already been realized.
This year he identified over one hundred that had already
come true!

Who was George Orwell? Born Eric Blair in India in 1903,
he had an upper-middle-class education in British private
schools where he avidly read ghost stories, Utopian books,
and particularly H. G. Wells. Though he early wanted to
write, he returned to India to serve in the Imperial Police
for five years. Back in England, he began to write mediocre
novels, fought and was wounded in the Spanish Civil War
(where he lost his early enchantment with communism), and
then worked out World War II at BBC and the *London Times*,
where his wartime London became the backdrop of *1984*.

Under the influence of political theorist James Burnham, he came to believe the world was moving to a managerial society of two classes, the poor and the ruling elite. In 1944 he first rose to prominence with his book, *The Animal Farm,* satirizing Russian communism. He then began *1984* in 1945 and completed the final draft in 1948. It was published in 1949; he died in 1950.

Orwell's forecasts have so far been uncannily accurate, many realized or even exceeded years before his estimate, making credible the possibility, at least, of the final totalitarian denouement. Let us look at a few.

ORWELL'S SCIENTIFIC AND TECHNOLOGICAL PREDICTIONS

Goodman divided Orwell's scientific and technological predictions into three classes:

1. Military Science

Since WWII scientists in the service of the military have doggedly kept pace with Orwell's imagination: today, not one of the ideas listed is beyond contemporary capabilities.

Let's look at a few of these "Predictions in Military Science":

a. Think tanks where experts plan future wars
b. Improved missiles and bombs
c. Planes independent of earth
d. Lenses suspended in space
e. Floating fortresses to guard important sea lanes
f. Germs immunized against all antibodies
g. Self-propelled bombs to take the place of bombing planes
h. Earthquake and tidal wave control
i. Efficient defoliants that could be spread over wide areas
j. Soil submarines that could bore through the ground

Goodman ominously concludes:

A nuclear explosion could easily infuse society with the siege mentality and war hysteria that the Oceania government adapted to its purposes.

2. Police Science

Here Orwell predicted:

a. Data banks containing detailed personal information
b. Rapid access to and retrieval of data
c. Two-way, flush-mounted televisions
d. Remote sensor of heartbeat
e. Tone-of-voice analyzer
f. Sensitive omnidirectional microphone
g. Police patrol helicopters
h. Large telescreens for public viewing
i. Memory holes for rapid destruction of information
j. Scanners to detect and analyze human thought

3. Finally, Psychoscience

All told, Orwell managed to foresee some of the most important devices of the last three decades. But nowhere was his foresight sharper than in the field of psychoscience. In Oceania, no man's thoughts are inviolate. The Thought Police can tell from a person's friendships, his relaxations, his behavior toward his wife and children, and the expression on his face when he is alone, the words he mutters in sleep, even characteristic movements of his body, whether he is being faithful to the Party. After identifying a dissident, the Thought Police use drugs, electric shock, and intricate forms of mental and physical torture to force a person to conform to Party norms.

In recent years, the science of psychoscience has gone even beyond that of *1984*. Since 1963 the number of brain scientists has increased tenfold to more than 6,000. In the U.S., the Bureau of Narcotics, the Department of Justice, and the CIA have become new sources of research funds. The broadening interface of academic science and government control has already begun spilling into the laboratory from the pages of *1984*.

More than 3,000 therapies to modify behavior are now recognized. Many suggest little more than transmogrified torture. Even Orwell's most frightening treatment, a prolonged and intimate contact with a dreaded phobic stimulus has been brought into modern therapy under the name of implosion or "flooding."

His conclusion concerning Orwell's scientific and technological predictions is that:

The possibility of Orwell's *1984* becoming reality --
perhaps even before the date he specified -- is clear.

ORWELL'S SOCIAL AND POLITICAL PREDICTIONS

The social trends of the last 30 years have brought
the West closer to *1984* than ever before, and these
trends could rapidly accelerate under certain circumstances,

says Goodman.

Here again, let's analyze a few:

1. "Doublethink" -- the glossing over of ugly reality
with contradictory ideological abstractions.

2. Denial of objective reality by insisting that reality
exists only in the human mind. Goodman sees this both in
the drug and alcohol cultures, and in the politicians backing policies unrelated to real needs.

3. Newspeak was the *1984* dictator's denigrating of the
English language so that heretical thoughts could not even
be verbalized -- seen, Goodman believes, in bureaucratic
gobbledy-gook and such neologisms as calling aggressive
bombing raids, "protective reactionary strikes"!

4. Orwell goes on to forecast from the totalitarian
state of *1984* today's practices of rewriting history to meet
political expediency, the political practice of exalting a
benevolent "Big Brother is watching over you" to unify confidence (TV newsmen may be an American type), continuous war
policies reflected in 1978's arms races, the breakup of the
family, and unwarranted search and surveillance of private
citizens, et al.

Again, Goodman concludes:

Not one of Orwell's predictions is beyond the range
of possibility, and almost any of the social and political trends described above could be brought to a head
by just a single triggering incident.

The "triggering incident" of which he speaks could be any
one of several. One such might be a terrorist group armed
with atomic weapons.

Regrettably, the evidence suggests that nuclear technology now is sufficiently diffused that such a contin-
gency is well within the realm of possibility.

For example, a professor at a large American university announced last summer that he had devised a way to
immensely simplify the separation of uranium isotopes.
By using a carbon dioxide laser, enough weaponsgrade
U^{235} for a bomb could be produced in about a year;   the
critical mass for U^{235}, when encased in a beryllium
neutron reactor, is only 11 kilograms. The professor
pointed out that the cost, approximately $100,000, is
within the capabilities of many small organizations.

Alarming is the realization that certain "triggering
incidents" could make Orwell's future a probable one.
In fact, these triggering incidents might even make the
world of *1984* a preferable future, because eternal warfare and a loss of liberty would be viewed as the price
that must be paid to avoid catastrophic destruction.

If terrorists actually exploded an atomic weapon
somewhere in the Western world, the willingness of people to give up their liberties would greatly intensify.
A nuclear explosion could easily infuse society with
the siege mentality and war hysteria that the Oceania
government adapts to its purposes. Some suggestion of
what might happen is the state of virtual warfare that
prevailed in Italy during the kidnapping of former
Premier Aldo Moro.

By actually exploding a nuclear weapon, terrorists
could destroy almost the entire government of a major
country. The result could be a power vacuum that
would be filled by either the most powerful insurgent
group fighting to gain control or by the group most
desiring of power. In neither case would there likely
be an overriding concern for individual rights.

Thus a future similar to that of *1984*, where survival is bought only at the price of subservience,
could come on schedule if terrorists gain access to
atomic weapons in the years before 1984.

Goodman finally concludes:

> The possibility of Orwell's *1984* becoming reality --
> perhaps even before the date he specified -- is clear.
> Whether or not it really happens will depend on what
> we do today. We must prepare to act on two fronts --
> to prevent the triggering incidents from taking place
> and to reverse the social trends that are leading the
> Western democracies towards *1984*.

He then suggests:

> An approach that might form a viable starting point
> for an initiative to prevent *1984* conditions is the
> suggestion of biophysicist and futurist John Platt
> that the countries of the world establish Councils of
> Urgent Studies. These councils would study what Platt
> calls the "crisis of crises" -- the flood of world
> problems that are occurring simultaneously in the cur-
> rent age of transformation. In doing this, they would
> have to give immediate attention to the specific
> crises that could lead to *1984*.

> Platt's councils would have two main tasks: first,
> to identify and appraise potential problems before
> they become uncontrollable, and, second, to solve them.

We ask: Is this probable -- or even possible, given the
records of the League of Nations, the UN, and other such
well-meaning but relatively impotent bodies? Paul Henry
Spaak, former Belgian President of the Council of Europe and
General Secretary of NATO, offered another solution a very
few years ago:

> The world in its present state needs a superman to
> direct or resolve its many difficult problems. No one
> knows who he will be or where he will come from but
> one thing is certain -- *he will soon make his appear-
> ance, and we are waiting for him!*

May George Orwell and Paul Spaak whet your appetite to
plunge into "The Evangelical Agenda -- 1984 and Beyond"!

In Search of Noah's Faith

Leighton Ford

It has been one year since we gathered together in Atlanta.

In a few days we will learn who *Time Magazine* has selected as the Man or Woman of 1978. Who do you think it might be? The test-tube baby? President Sadat or Prime Minister Begin? Muhammad Ali? Jimmy Carter? Or perhaps Howard Jarvis? All made the *Time* cover this year.

But what if God were selecting His man or woman of the year -- whom would He choose? A clue may come from a past generation, when man's evil was running rampant, and God found one righteous man who was walking with Him. I would like to suggest, as we consider the future, that we take Noah as our model.

It is interesting to speculate how we as evangelicals might go about building the ark in the 1970's:

-- Ham, Shem, and Japheth would each be asked to write books about their experiences (for different publishing companies); possible titles might be - "Hammering Out Your Identity" - "When Life Turns into a Zoo" -- and (with permission from our good friend, Marabel Morgan) - "The Total Sailor."

-- someone would certainly write a book on Noah as an example of how to handle your money; after all, he was the only man who was able to keep his "stock" afloat when the rest of the world was in liquidation.

-- a mail-order firm would send out letters to at least twelve different mailing lists urging readers to "build your own family ark ... be a testimony to your neighborhood ... send for a set of plans and get pre-cut gopher wood for $2,499.95. We accept check, money order, Visa or Master Charge."

-- a Christian rock group would undoubtedly record an album about the ark. Some possible selections: "Seasick but Safe" - "Animals Got More Sense than Folks" - "The Lord's Gonna' Close the Door."

-- a whole series of new magazines would be published - "The Ark Today" - "The Reformed Ark" - "Seafarers" - and, of course, "The Ararat Door."

-- there would be conferences on "how to build bigger arks" - counter-conferences on "how to build simpler arks" - with side consultations on "how to contextualize ark build-ing."

-- once a month Noah would stop building and have a fund-raising "telethon," offering splinters of the ark as a give-away.

-- in fact, there is a good possibility that Noah wouldn't even have time to build the ark today, because he'd be so busy on the banquet and talk-show circuit. With a novel idea like an ark, we would latch onto him in a minute as a "per-sonality." Can't you just hear the introduction: "Five years ago Noah wasn't even thinking about row boats; now, since he began following the Lord, he is building the Queen Mary of ancient Babylon!"

You will please pardon my tongue-in-cheek scenario for a modern-day Noah. If we wanted to, it would be easy to poke fun at foibles like these in most of our organizations. But seriously, I believe that Noah can be a model for us. There has been a rash of books and movies today about the search for Noah's ark. What we need far more, is to be in search of Noah's *faith*. Noah is a biblical hero because he was faithful. The significance of his faith is more important than the location of his ark, impressive as it would be to find the ark.

The Scriptures do not put the emphasis on the flood, or
the ark, but on *Noah*. Ezekiel 14 names Noah as one of three
righteous men whose exceptional merit might atone for others'
sins if anyone could. Our Lord Jesus in Luke 17 declared,

> As it was in the days of Noah, so it will be in the days
> of the Son of Man. They ate, they drank, they married,
> they were given in marriage, until the day when Noah
> entered into the ark and the flood came, and destroyed
> them all.

Noah, the lonely, righteous figure, stands between the sinful
and unheeding world, going on with business as usual, and
ultimate judgment. Peter adds a further note when he describes Noah as a "herald of righteousness" (II Peter 2).

Hebrews 11 singles out Noah as the man whose future-
oriented faith leads him to active obedience,

> By faith, Noah, when warned about things not yet seen,
> in holy fear, built an ark to save his family. By his
> faith he condemned the world and became heir of the
> righteousness that comes by faith. (Hebrews 11:7)

By faith, Noah did exactly what God said. He staked his future on the sheer word of God without any external evidence.
For 120 years, he went through the daily routine of living a
godly life in an ungodly environment. During that time there
was no recognition, no speaking tours, no money coming in
from his books and projects. But faith and faithfulness in
the ordinariness of daily living prepared Noah for the cata-
clysmic moment, the day of opportunity.

What if God told us this week to build an ocean liner in
Kansas City! Imagine 120 years of ridicule and scorn with
no rain in Missouri! What faith this must have taken! But
faith is the evidence of what is not seen, the willingness
to go out on a limb for God's Word!

When we come as Christians to a conference on the future,
we have a problem. Few of us have expertise as futurists.
And as the Chinese proverb reminds us, prophesying is very
difficult -- especially about the future.

A review in the *The Futurist* magazine lists a number of
"prognostic boo-boos" in the past. In 1899, *Literary Digest*
predicted that the "'horseless carriage' would never come into as 'common use' as a bicycle!" In 1902, *Harper's Weekly*

said, "the actual building of roads devoted to motor cars is
not for the near future." *Science Digest* prophesied in 1948
that "landing and moving around the moon offers so many serious problems that it may take science another 200 years to
lock them."

Which futurists should we believe? The alarmists or the
pessimists? Those who see a long future for mankind? Or
those who believe our time is short? Some Christians believe
we ought to plan for two or three hundred years ahead; others
say we may hardly have any time left.

It seems to me we must be somewhat wary of extrapolation
-- the projection of trends -- lest we fall into the idolatry
of statistics. The Gallup Poll may tell us that there are
more born-again Christians than ever before and that there
has been an upsurge in the influence of religion in America.
But if conditions change, there can be a certain apostasy, a
falling away. We can also be paralyzed into an unbiblical
determinism by the trends highlighted in the media. We can
moan at the progress of evil and decay. But is it not possible for God to break in and intervene as He has done in the
great revivals in the past? Is the God who sits on the
throne no longer able to say, "Behold, I make all things new"?

Whether we have many years or few, our main concern in
every generation is to look to the infallible word of our God
as our guide, not only for the ultimate wrap-up of history
but how to redeem the time in the intervening years. While
discerning all we can of trends in the world around us, we
are called, above all, to believe and to obey the Word of God.

And here Noah still speaks to us.

Noah's faith led him to obey God, and in holy fear to
build an ark to save his family. The big question is not,
where are we on the time line, but are we faithfully sounding the prophetic alarm to the world and the church? I wonder whether we do not need to recover a new consciousness of
the coming flood.

The ark was not a novel idea to communicate the faith.
It was no gimmick, but a matter of life and death. Noah was
convinced of this, and we, too, are not to ask people to get
into the ark only because Christ offers a better life or more
comfortable life (what He offers may be more uncomfortable).
We offer salvation because it is the *only life*, the *only* escape from the flood. Ultimately, we need to test every min-

istry by asking: does this ministry proclaim the death of
death and hell's destruction?

The story of Noah is a serious warning to those of us who
are Christian workers. The old Scottish divine, Alexander
Whyte once wrote,

> Every ax stroke and the echo of every hammer was a
> louder and ever louder call to the men of that corrupt
> and violent day to flee from the wrath to come, but
> sad to say, the very men without whose help the ark
> would never have been built failed to take passage on
> that ship for themselves and for their wives and for
> their children ... all Noah's own excellent sermons
> would not have kept his gray head above the rising
> waters he so often described in his sermons had he not
> himself done what the Lord commanded him to do.

How seriously do we take the warning of God and the salvation of God for ourselves -- and our families -- and our children? Alexander Whyte imagined the reason only eight people
were saved, as a result of Noah's preaching, was that his sons
and daughters undid all their father's preaching, especially
Ham! A sober concern of this conference ought to be signs of
family breakdown among evangelicals, even divorces among evangelical leaders. What will this mean to the next generation?

We preachers often use the story of Noah as an evangelistic
symbol. We urge our hearers to "get into the ark before the
door is closed." But there is also a key social message in
the story of Noah: like Enoch, Noah walked with God, and,
walking with God, he was out of step with the world.   In
fact, by building the ark he "condemned the world."

This "social significance of faith" is underlined by Peter
in his first epistle. The believers of Peter's day were suffering under an official policy of persecution. Peter reminds them of the story of Noah, and how, in the ark, a few
people, eight in all, were "saved through water." God brought
them out of an evil world, through the flood of judgment, into
safety. Just so, for believers in Peter's day, baptism was a
sign of their deliverance out of the world. Through the resurrection, says Peter, Jesus has overcome the hostile spirits
who lie behind the official persecution. Believers, like Noah
and his family, are saved out of the web of the world's sin
and delivered from the bitter effects of ungodliness.

The early church used the ark on stormy seas as a symbol
of the church. Why? Because God saves His people out of the
world before He uses them to rebuild it.

Deliverance out of the world is not the whole truth of salvation. Believers are also sent into the world to witness to
it, but --

-- judgment comes before mercy
-- wrath before the new covenant
-- the flood before the rainbow.

This is the message of Noah.

One translation of Genesis 6 makes the point:

God, seeing that the misdeeds of men were multiplied
on earth and the thoughts of his heart were continually bent on evil ... was grieved inwardly with sorrow. *But there was Noah ...*

Noah was the exception, the nonconformist. Noah shows us
that the people of faith ought to be the conscience of the
world. They are to be the watchmen of the world who see the
enemy approaching and sound the warning alarm. But they are
also to be the pioneers of the new covenant. No matter how
evil things are, they will not surrender hope. And there
lies the difference between the prophet and the cynic.

Recently my wife and I went with some friends to see Hal
Holbrook's marvelous re-creation of Mark Twain. It was a
stunning one-man performance. During the evening Holbrook
characterized the passage of Mark Twain from a whimsical hu-
morist, poking fun at the foibles of mankind, into a bitter
old man whose soul had been corroded.

Twain rails at mankind's hypocrisy in a way that is almost
prophetic. He calls upon God in a make-believe pulpit prayer
to "kill those bloody bastards -- in a spirit of love." But
because he has no hope of redemption, Twain ends up as cynic,
not as prophet.

He concludes his tragic performance by asking,

Is man really the noblest creation of God? Than I
would like to see the ignoblest. Is humanity a joke?
Did God put man together on a dull day? Did God make
man because He was disappointed with monkeys? I would

like to get mankind back on the ark again -- with an
augur! When I get to the other side, I am going to
use all my influence to put humanity through the flood
again, and not make any mistakes this time -- not even
have an ark.

By his faith Noah was saved from cynicism and became an
heir of righteousness. After the flood came the rainbow.
After the judgment came the message of hope. After the deluge Noah became the founder of a new civilization, the first
mediator of the universal covenant between God and man. What
went into the ark was not only eight souls, but a whole new
world in microcosm, all the furniture, so to speak, for the
next stage of the Kingdom of God. The story of Noah teaches
us that only those who take seriously both evil and the judgment of God can really hope for a new world.

This year our agenda calls for us to look, not just at the
world's future, but especially at the mission of the church
in the intermediate future. The question before us is, "Do
we know how to build an ark? We know how to build schools,
and buildings, and television networks, and organizations,
and mailing lists. But do we know what the ark of God
should look like? Have we been paying attention to the
Architect's drawings?"

Is the church supposed to be a lifeboat to rescue drowning
souls? Or is the church supposed to be a landing craft meant
to carry the seeds of a new social order? I am suggesting
Noah as a model because he typifies our responsibility.

As he prepared the ark in which people could be saved, he
had an evangelistic ministry. As he stood out from the evils
of his age, his lifestyle gave him a prophetic ministry.

The illustration of Noah is in line with the scriptural
revelation about the place of the church in God's cosmic plan.

We will need to pay close attention to Dr. Clowney's studies from the book of Ephesians. For in Ephesians Paul shows
the church as more than the *agent of evangelism*, though it is
that; and more than an agent of *social change*, though, in a
very special sense, it is that; but as the agent of God's
entire cosmic purpose.

The church as seen in Ephesians is not primarily an institution, but redeemed people. There is an institutional side
of the church, just as God gave Noah careful dimensions for

the ark. But Noah and his family were more important than
the ark.

Ephesians 2:8-10 makes clear that the church is, first of
all, to be the redeemed community of those who have been saved
by grace through faith. And we are redeemed in order to do
the good works which God has prepared for us. Like Noah, we
are to walk with God as a righteous people, to build the ark
and to do the good works which God has planned for us. Like
him, we are to have both a prohetic and an evangelistic ministry. Howard Snyder puts it well, "Evangelism and prophecy
are the positive and negative charges of the church's spiritual power."

Here again, we have both the flood and the rainbow. That
same balance is seen in John 17, where Jesus prays that His
disciples might be holy and one in order that they might go
into the world and the world might believe.

Now against the background of this story and its initial
truths, I would like to suggest some questions that we might
ask ourselves during this week. I don't know whether there
will be another conference like this next year. But let's
think about how we would evaluate the situation if those of
us in this room should meet, God willing, ten years from now.

What would have happened in our evangelistic ministries?
Like Noah, we are to herald the righteousness and salvation
of God. As God in His patience waited in Noah's day for 120
years, so He is not willing that any should perish today.
He delays the return of Christ until the message of salvation
is carried to the ends of the world. As God told Noah to be
fruitful and multiply, so He expects His people to grow until
the church is planted and disciples made among every people
on the earth.

What will happen to those Americans who George Gallup believes are "spiritually homeless" -- "searching for deeper
meaning in their lives"? Will the one-third of the American
people who claim to be born again be disciples ten years
from now? Will they be following Jesus Christ as Lord in a
community of Christ's people? We dare not complacently look
at America only through the lenses of the Gallup Poll; we
must look at them through the lenses of discipleship and not
be content until people who now call themselves "evangelicals"
are part of a community of believers and involved in the work
of the Kingdom.

What about the 80 million Americans who make up the unchurched? Lutheran Professor J. Russell Hale has done a
landmark study (*Who Are the Unchurched?*) which ought to be
required reading for all of us. He spent six months in six
of the most unchurched counties in America, asking people
who did not go to church, "Why not?" And the message that
came through loud and clear was: most of these people had
heard much more bad news than good news in the churches they
had attended; most of them had never heard of a God who loved
them and who could, for Christ's sake, receive and forgive
them as they are now. How many of these 80 million will have
been reached by 1988? What will your church and organization
and mine have done to reach them?

What about the young adults of this country? The great
population bulge in the next ten years will be those twenty-
five to forty-five years of age. These are the people who
have grown up with *Playboy Magazine*, and who have been most
affected by the cult of self-worship. These are the people
who have been taught to be lovers of pleasure, lovers of self,
lovers of money, rather than lovers of God. Psychologist Paul
Vitz describes these young adults as living basically for career and consumerism. Vitz believes their philosophy of self-
ism is going to be running out within the decade. "In another
ten years," he predicts, "millions of people will be bored
with the cult of self and will be looking for a new life ...
the uncertainty is not the existence of this coming wave of
returning prodigals, but whether their Father's house, the
true faith, will still be there to welcome and celebrate
their return." What will your church and your organization
and mine have done in the next ten years to reach out and
welcome these young adults?

Ralph Winter will lay before us this week the 2.4 billion
of the world's peoples who have never yet heard enough about
Jesus Christ to make an intelligent choice about Him. He will
tell us, I am sure, our missionary agencies are putting most
of their money and time into areas already reached. He will
challenge us to a kind of wartime commitment and self-
sacrifice. In June 1980, the Consultation on World Evangelization sponsored by the Lausanne Committee will meet in Thai-
land. It will ask the question, "How shall they hear?" ...
Buddhists and Marxists and Muslims and other unreached peoples? Let me ask: if the priorities of your church and organization and mine develop in a straight line from present
priorities and plans ... if there is no creative and imagina-
tive re-allocating of resources, how many of these 2.4 billion
will have heard and become disciples -- how many will be on

the way to heaven and how many on the way to hell -- ten years from now?

And what about the so-called "electric church," the vast enterprise of programming the Gospel on radio and TV? Martin Marty fears the "electric church" is creating a generation of spectator Christians, while Ben Armstrong holds that the media now take worship and evangelism to the home and lives of ordinary people as the early Christians did. What effects do we believe present trends in mass-media evangelism will have on the life and strength of local churches in the next ten years? Are there changes we believe can and should take place?

Evangelization could alter in the next ten years, suffering from the idolatry of methodology on one hand, or the paralysis of analysis on the other. We could choose to pour our energies into one particular approach to reach the world, perhaps overlooking the cultural and spiritual insensitivity which this involves. Or we could get hung up in statistical post mortems of evangelistic efforts which, if taken to the extreme, could paralyze us into inaction.

It's noteworthy that Noah's ark never started a fad! As far as we know, no one ever tried to duplicate the ark. I suggest that the answers to these questions about our evangelistic ministry will not depend on gimmicks, but on how well we rediscover the basics of spiritual warfare -- of holy living, of the equipping of the body of believers, of costly and loving outreach, of faithful proclamation of the whole work of God, of spirit-filled prayer to God and communication to men.

What will happen in ten years in terms of our prophetic ministry?

As Noah was a sign to his generation, so the church is called to be a sign of the Kingdom in the world.

In ten years will anyone be saying that the "born again" movement produced men and women whose lives exhibit the rule of God? "We must ask the question," says George Gallup, "Are our churches producing 'nice' people or 'new' people?"

Charles Colson asks, "Why does it seem that the secular world offers abundant evidence that religion is not greatly affecting our lives?" "Is it," he wonders, "that we have so accommodated the Gospel of Jesus Christ to twentieth-century humanism that what we offer is no more than a better way for man to achieve his humanistic goals?"

A member of this Consultation in a recent letter suggests that the Gospel that is being sold today "promises maximum blessing with minimum pain, and sees the ark of God as the route to escape rather than a prophetic statement."

Is he right?

Ten years from now, will our salt have any more bite than it does today?

Missionary anthropologist, Don Jacobs, has written about the relation of conversion to non-Christian cultures in a way that contains helpful lessons for the evangelical situation in America today. He points out that Christian groups go through three phases in relationship to their culture: a phase of rejection, followed by a phase of accommodation, and then a third stage marked by the re-establishment of identity.

During the first stage, in which converts reject their culture, sharp lines are drawn between the believer and the world. Then, in the second phase, evangelism becomes primary. Since evangelism requires communication, Christians, in a sense, have to rejoin society. The sharp edges of separation tend to be dulled. This is a significant period if evangelism is to be effective. At the same time, it is a period of theological peril, especially in the temptation to syncretism. The Christian community tries to accommodate its own values to the community around. It is an era in which political rapprochement takes place and converts are expected to be responsible citizens as well as dedicated Christians.

It seems to me that the evangelical movement in the United States has been going through this pattern. In the last generation we have moved out of the phase of rejection into a time of great evangelistic outreach. Now we may be on the border line between this second phase of evangelism and accommodation, and stage three, the new search for identity. In stage three, says Jacobs, "symbols of separation are again sought ... the Christian communities decide for themselves what battles they feel compelled to fight. Usually they choose some social evil which they feel threatens their Christian values." (Battle lines have been drawn this year over homosexual rights and the encroachment of government on religious schools.)

This third era also has great potential for division. Christians don't always move at the same speed or on the same

issues. A new radical rejection movement may arise on the
fringes and demand that converts display the new subculture's
chosen signs of separation. Another group moves in the direction of even more accommodation and may end up losing most of
the radical demands of the Gospel and requiring only symbolic
rituals and dues from converts.

This movement seems to apply to evangelicals in America
today. Along with the success of our evangelism and the public emergence of evangelicalism, have come divisions along
radical and accommodational lines. It seems to me, therefore, that one of the major questions before this Consultation is: how do we faithfully respond to this situation?
How do we identify the true enemies of the Gospel? How do
we recognize those who, though they may be different on some
issues, are our true blood brothers and sisters? How do we
identify the signs of conversion which speak prophetically
to our era?

In a word, what are the "brandmarks" of Jesus?

We may not agree on what are the most crucial public issues, but can we not agree that for the church of Jesus Christ
the most crucial issue is whether we will be, as John Stott
entitles his book on the Sermon on the Mount, a true "counter-
culture"?

Ten years from now, will "born again" Christians be hungering and thirsting after righteousness in our lives and society more than today? Or will we be hungering and coveting
more after the comforts of success and affluence?

Ten years from now, will we be more peacemakers than we are
today, helping to defuse the anger and hostility that explodes
into violence, into battered children, and broken lives?

Ten years from now, will we be more pure in heart, or more
infected with the sexual lusts around us?

Ten years from now, will evangelical families have more
divorces, or be more known for family fidelity?

Ten years from now, will we be known to the world and each
other as people of integrity, who mean it when we say, "Yes"
or "No," and who can be counted on to keep our promises? Or
will we, too, leave behind a trail of broken vows?

Ten years from now, if anti-evangelical feeling rises, will
we be known for loving our enemies, even as we disagree with
them? If our theology is better than "theirs" (whoever "they"
are), will the grace of the Lord Jesus truly shine forth
through us as the light of the world?

And, finally, who is this "we" that all of us will be talking about all week? Who are we "evangelicals"? Do we see
ourselves and those we represent as the total picture of what
God is doing? Or do we see evangelicalism as a renewal task
force destined to quicken all the scattered fragments of the
body of Christ? In other words, are we prepared to recognize
all those who are "in the ark" of salvation as our brothers
and sisters?

Howard Snyder believes that "evangelical Christianity today is more than a group of theologically conservative
churches" and that it "could become a worldwide movement ...
a thoroughly biblical evangelical movement that includes
Catholic, Protestant, Orthodox and Jewish Christians." If
there is any hope for Snyder's dream -- and we all know how
deep and hard are the theological questions which such a suggestion raises -- but if there is any substance to what he
says, how will we respond in the next ten years?

How are we, for example, to relate to the twenty percent
of American Roman Catholics who now say that they, too, are
evangelicals? Billy Graham has had the door opened again
this year to preach in Eastern Europe. In Poland the Catholic
churches were made available for him in which to preach, and
hundreds of Catholics responded. The head of a Catholic theological college told him how he had been born again while
studying in Chicago. And hundreds of inquirers are being
followed up through an evangelically-oriented Catholic Bible
study fellowship known as Oasis. What kind of friendship, of
nurture, of dialogue, of acceptance and encouragement does
God want us to offer to Catholic "evangelicals"?

What kind of commitment are we prepared to give to the support of worldwide structures for evangelical communication and
cooperation? I think immediately of the Lausanne continuation
committee, which I am privileged to chair, and which has become an increasingly vital symbol and resource for cooperation
in evangelization, especially to our brothers and sisters in
the Third World. We deeply need your prayers, advice, and
support. I think also of the World Evangelical Fellowship,
with roots that go back a century. It seems to me an utter
tragedy that at this very moment of unparalleled evangelical

opportunity, WEF's executive secretary, Waldron Scott, has
had to give up his office and work out of his home and spend
most of his time struggling to raise an almost absurdly minimal budget. What does that say about our commitment to work
together to build the ark worldwide?

I don't have the answers to these questions; I do feel the
need to discuss them.

Well, my brothers and sisters, we have come together these
days to observe the signs of the times, to watch for the gathering clouds of judgment, to look for the rainbow of promise,
and to hear the word of God.

I have just come from a crusade in Niagara Falls, New York,
a community that has been depressed economically and spiritually for a generation or two. And we had a wonderful week as
God's people joined together to reach out in evangelism.

They call this city by the thundering Niagara river,
"Rainbow Country."

And I could not help thinking of the vision in Revelation 10, of a mighty angel coming down out of heaven. He put
his right foot on the sea and his left on the land. He had
a small scroll open in his hand. He spoke with a loud voice
that sounded like the roar of lions. He proclaimed God's
message to the nations. He was wrapped in a cloud, and
around his head ... was a rainbow.

My prayer for this week is that God would help us all to
be like that angel ... with our minds set on heaven ... with
our feet firmly planted in the realities of this world ...
with the Word of God in our hand ... with the message of
God's grace and judgment sounding firmly from our lips ...
and with the rainbow of God's promise, like latter-day Noahs,
shining over our lives!

PART II

Addresses and Responses

A Utopian Perspective on the Future

Address: Willis W. Harman

Social and historical forces are gathered to bring about a great transformation of industrialized society. To say that is not to assume the transformation is preordained; only that it could come about. Other outcomes are possible. The strains on the social order could prove to be too much, and the whole thing might collapse. Or anxiety might predominate and society might opt for a highly authoritarian order. The signs we see might prove to be a mirage, and the transformation abortive.

It is neither utopian nor dystopian to see these alternative possibilities. Perhaps it is utopian to imagine that the transformation might take place smoothly and that trans-industrial society might have some very desirable characteristics.

Underneath the frenetic activity of daily events and the slower movements of institutional change, there lie still deeper patterns of deeper cultural characteristics. These change only slowly through the centuries. Nonetheless, any serious study of the future must take them into account for they shape the changes at the more rapidly varying levels.

At this deep level of the societal structure every society forms around some basic paradigm, some tacitly assumed set of fundamental beliefs about man, society, the universe, and the source of authority. Very rarely in history has this basic worldview gone through rapid and fundamental change. Lewis Mumford, in his *Transformations of Man*, estimates less

than a half-dozen such transformations in the entire history
of Western civilization, the last one being the ending of the
Middle Ages. He reminds us how dramatic was the value shift
involved: "All but one of the seven deadly sins, sloth, was
transformed into a positive virtue. Greed, avarice, envy,
gluttony, luxury, and pride were the driving forces of the
new economy." In the realm of beliefs, the shift from the
medieval perception of a cosmos alive in every portion to the
post-seventeenth-century scientific view of regular phenomena
in a "dead" universe devoid of mental or spiritual properties
was equally dramatic. All institutions in society were inti-
mately involved in these changes, both being shaped by the
evolving worldview and also helping to shape it.

We have seen, particularly in the last two decades, evidences that the long-term trends of modernization, including
evolution of both worldview and institutions, may be turning
in a new direction. There is some reason to think that this
could happen with what in historical terms is extraordinary
rapidity, and that we may be living through a period of great
wrenching during which it will be particularly important to
understand what is going on, and to develop the ability to
ride with the transformational currents.

THE LONG-TERM MULTIFOLD MODERNIZATION TREND

The centuries-old multifold modernization trend which
started in Western Europe some eight or ten centuries ago
has since spread to affect practically all the peoples of
the globe. It involves a number of component trends, of
which the most fundamental started with a shift in basic
cultural beliefs and values:

-- Secularization of values -- that is, the tendency to
   organize activities rationally around impersonal and
   utilitarian values and patterns, rather than having
   these prescribed by social and religious tradition;
   leading to and associated with the concept of material progress.

From this root belief-system change stem a number of other
component trends, of which some of the most important are:

-- Industrialization of the production of goods and
   services -- and eventually of more and more of human activities, in the process changing the quality
   of those goods and services, and also of the work
   involved in producing them

-- Economic rationalization of social behavior and organization -- including the tendency for all things
to become measurable by and purchasable with dollars,
and the growing predominance of economic rational-
ity in social and political decisionmaking

-- "Technification" of knowledge -- that is, the tendency to consider as important that knowledge which
is useful in generating manipulative technology,
and to downplay claims that there can be an important body of knowledge about wholesome human values
and goals, personal growth and development, and
spiritual aspirations

-- Increasing per-capita impact on the physical environment and per-capita use of resources

-- Increasing centralization, bigness

-- Specialization, impersonalization of roles

etc.

This fundamental multi-component trend is inherent in the
institutions of modern industrialized society; its persever-
ance is implicitly assumed in most projections of the future.
Yet there is impressive evidence that a trend-change is not
only possible but may be well underway. This evidence of the
plausibility of incipient transformation is of four kinds:

-- Social movements which amount, in the aggregate, to
a broad countertrend force, and which include a vision of a different future than the modernization
trend would lead toward

-- Basic contradictions in modern society which create
pressure for restructuring

-- Historic indicators of approaching revolutionary
change being presently visible

-- Basic premises underlying the form of modern society
showing signs of undergoing fundamental change.

SOCIAL MOVEMENTS

Since the early 1960's numerous social movements have become visible which can be interpreted as protests against one

or more of the component trends identified above, and as af-
firmations of a "New Age" society. These include a wide variety of specific focuses such as appropriate technology, en-
vironmentalist, conservationist, holistic health, person liberation, feminist, technology assessment, voluntary simplicity, human potential, "new transcendentalism," and numerous
others. The following table shows how these various and diverse movements can be interpreted as a countertrend force
tending to deflect society from continuing along the path of
further "modernization."

LONG-TERM MODERNIZATION TREND AND COUNTERTREND COMPONENTS

Trend	Countertrend
Basic	
Secularization	"New transcendentalism"; quest for meanings
Industrialization	Reaction against "industri- alization" of education, health care, agriculture, etc.
Economic rationalization	Reaction against dominance of economic rationality over ethics, social rationality, human values
"Technification" of knowledge	Search for knowledge of human values and goals
Derivative	
Technological, economic, and material growth	"Limits-to-growth" arguments; proposed change in qualita- tive nature of growth emphasis
Increasing use of inan- imate energy sources	Energy conservation, "con- server society" movements
Increasing institution- ization of innovation	Challenge to "technological imperative"; technology as- sessment movement
Increasing bigness of technology, centraliza- tion	"Small is beautiful", appro- priate technology, decentral- ization movements

Trend	Countertrend
Urbanization	Reruralization movement
Increasing impact on environment	Environmentalist movements, rise of ecological ethic
Increasing power of weapons	Nuclear disarmament movement
Movement toward a single world economy	Small-country-self-determination movements, demands for "reshaping the international order"
Increasing specialization, influence of technical elite	Politization of scientific and technical decisions, with public participation; "defrocking" of the experts
Tendency for ties binding individual to institutions to become impersonal	New emphasis on community, family values, human relationships, human potential movement, person-liberation
Acquisitive materialism as the mainspring	Voluntary simplicity movements

We are speaking here about industrialized societies, but a counterpart to the countertrend movement is to be found in the Third World in the form of a "liberatory development" movement offering an alternative to economic development in the sense of striving to become like Western (or Communist) industrialized societies. "Liberatory" development would place the emphasis on human liberation and well-being, self-reliance of developing peoples, and preservation of cultural values, rather than on strictly economic goals and mindless adoption of Western technology.

BASIC CONTRADICTIONS

Behind these social movements are some very real contradictions faced by modern industrialized societies. As examples consider the following five assumptions that tend to be taken for granted, but lead to questionable conclusions:

1. Fulfillment comes from the consumption of scarce resources. This assumption is woven through the structure of materialistic modern society; it underlies the standard economic indicators, the concept of economic growth, the idea of planned obsolescence. The dominant institution in modern

society is the economy, and the performance of the economy is
judged on the consumption of goods and services -- all of
which use up scarce resources and exude polluting waste. Hedonistic consumption, once a vice, is now promoted; frugality,
until recently a virtue, is now bad for the economy. Yet the
entropic handwriting on the wall is clear: frugal we must become. The consumption ethic leads inexorably to global competition and conflict of increasing proportions.

2. Employment is a byproduct of economic production. Thus
as industrialized societies face limits to the amount of production, while pressures continue to increase labor product-
ivity, meaningful work becomes a scarce commodity. But modern
society also rightly considers employment (i.e., satisfying
social roles) for its citizens to be essential to their well-
being. Employment in this sense is the individual's primary
relationship to society, through which (s)he makes a personal
contribution and receives affirmation in return, and in the
process builds essential self-esteem. The assumption that employment (jobs) is a mere byproduct of economic production is
in contradiction to this concern.

3. It is not practicable to ask the rich of the world to
decrease significantly their material standard of living to
redistribute to the poor. Yet they clearly cannot afford not
to. World distribution of food, income, and wealth is far
more uneven than is the distribution in any single country,
even those with the most notoriously unjust political orders.
Yet there seems to be no workable proposal to correct this
situation. Instead, economic and demographic forces conspire
to cause the maldistribution to grow steadily worse. The rich
"North" partakes of a feast that the world's limited resources
cannot sustain, while the teeming populations of the impover-
ished "South" remain trapped by poverty, illiteracy, and high
birth rates in a remorseless cycle of deprivation, and the
threat of ultimate "wars of redistribution" grows ever more
imminent.

4. Technology will solve social problems. Economic and
technological growth have brought abundance, problem-solving
capabilities, and have liberated humankind in numerous ways.
Yet in recent years technology has contributed to new kinds
of scarcity (e.g., of fresh air and water, of waste-absorbing
capacity of the environment); it has proven to be in some measure problem-generating; the institutions which house it are
accused of being enslaving. New and alarming democracy-
threatening aspects have begun to surface. For example, the
possibility of major dependence on nuclear power poses grave

threats to civil rights and liberties, such as the mandatory
psychiatric examinations proposed to insure the mental stability of persons having access to dangerous nuclear fuels
and waste. More fundamentally, the very momentum of economic
and technological growth leads toward the automatic making of
far-reaching social decisions (e.g., the growth imperative,
"autonomous technology"), in effect bypassing the political
process.

MODERNIZATION OUTCOMES

Abundance	⟶	Scarcity
Problem solving	⟶	Problem generating
Unintended benefits	⟶	Unintended detriments
Freeing	⟶	Enslaving
Democracy supporting	⟶	Democracy threatening

5. Science will produce the knowledge we need. Modern
society has developed science and technology that enable it
to accomplish feats which other societies could only dream
about. Yet it is clearly confused in matters of guiding values and ultimate goals. The deepest value commitments and
the ultimate goals of all societies that ever existed have
come from the profound inner experiences of some group of
people -- religious leaders, prophets, mystics, poet-
philosophers, or in some visionary cultures the majority of
the adult population. Some form of systematic knowledge of
the world of inner experience, publicly validated and widely
disseminated, would seem to be among the knowledge most needed
to guide society in its crucial choices. Yet modern society's
official knowledge system -- science -- tends to assume *a
priori* that these experiences will in the end be explained
(or explained away) as epiphenomena from a perishable brain,
and has steadfastly excluded these phenomena from its field
of study. The prevailing view in the culture is that such
systematization of, and consensus on, inner wisdom is im-
practicable.

HISTORIC INDICATORS

A third kind of evidence comes from sociological studies
of past periods of revolutionary change in various societies.
These studies indicate that typically there are precursors of
such fundamental transformations, in certain social indicators which rise some years prior to the revolutionary change
period and subsequently decline. These indicators include

alienation from the institutions of society; rate of mental
illness; rate of violent crime; rate of social disruption and
use of police to put down dissension; tolerance of hedonistic
behavior, particularly sexual; religious cultism; and economic
inflation. All of these indicators have risen since the mid-
Sixties

> REVOLUTIONARY CHANGE IN THE PAST
> HAS BEEN PRECEDED BY INCREASE IN:
>
> -- Alienation
>
> -- Rate of mental illness
>
> -- Rate of violent crime
>
> -- Incidence of social disruption
>
> -- Tolerance of sexual hedonism
>
> -- Religious cultism
>
> -- Economic inflation

CHANGE IN BASIC PREMISES

A fourth kind of evidence is particularly significant in
that it emphasizes how fundamental a change is taking place.
This is the evidence pointing to change in some of the most
basic, tacitly assumed premises in modern industrialized culture. New developments in biofeedback training, psychic research, and consciousness research indicate that a number of
the implicit premises underlying modern positivistic science
are challenged by the most recent findings of science itself.

> METAMORPHOSIS:
>
> Fundamental change of form
>
> METANOIA:
>
> Fundamental change of mind

Both in the culture at large, and in fringe areas in the
scientific community, the dominant science-technology paradigm
is being challenged in a fundamental sense. Survey data indicate a significant cultural shift in the direction of more
interest in spiritual and psychic matters, particularly among
the better educated. The challenge amounts to a reconsidera-
tion of the outmoded "warfare between science and religion"
(presumably won long ago by science, hands down). The growing suspicion is that traditional religion and conventional

science alike are both partial and flawed, and due to be
superseded by a more unified view of reality.

ONCE-TABOO SCIENTIFIC AREAS

-- Hypnosis

-- Unconscious processes

-- Psychosomatic illness

-- Sleep and dreams

-- Creativity

-- [Biofeedback training]

-- Psychic phenomena

-- States of consciousness

In fact, this development has been progressing for some
time. Once-taboo areas of science -- notably sleep and
dreams, creativity, hypnosis, unconscious processes, psychosomatic theories of illness -- have become legitimated. Psychic phenomena such as "remote viewing," precognition, and
psychokinesis are being explored with renewed interest.
Altered states of consciousness related to those tradition-
ally known by such terms as meditation, contemplation, and
"graces of interior prayer," are being tentatively explored
via biofeedback training and other routes.

The implications of these recent research findings in these
areas are paradigm-shaking indeed. Some representative examples are:

-- Unconscious knowing is far more extensive than ordinar-
ily assumed, and includes not only the sorts of knowledge of "involuntary" bodily processes brought to light
by biofeedback, but also unconscious knowledge of the
various realms of psychic phenomena

-- Because of the preponderance of the unconscious in our
mental processes, there are previously unsuspected
powers associated with beliefs, images, suggestions,
etc.

-- Mind is ultimately dominant over biological processes
(rather than being some sort of epiphenomenon deriving
from them)

-- Mind is extended in time and space (as evidenced by such
   phenomena as "remote viewing" and precognition)

-- Minds are joined, in ways other than the usually assumed
   physical mechanisms of communication

-- Mind is ultimately predominant over the physical world,
   as evidenced by psychokinetic phenomena

-- Thus the arguments by which an earlier generation of
   scientists had declared the fundamental tenets of religion to be illusion, turn out themselves to be invalid

-- Hence we are led to revised views of the possibility of
   knowing meaning in life, of transcendent goals for the
   individual and society, of the significance of "losing
   one's mind," of birth and death

THE POSSIBILITY OF A "NEW" SCIENCE

As physicists have learned to reconcile once-contradictory
wave and particle pictures of elemental physical stuff, so we
today are learning to reconcile inner and outer perceptions
of reality, and physical and spiritual aspects of human experience. This is no mere theoretical argument by the aca-
demics. All about us are signs of involvement of ordinary
people -- pursuing spiritual disciplines, adopting holistic
approaches to their own health care, becoming interested in
questions of death and dying, investigating the paranormal.
The culture is no longer so sure that fundamental concepts
of religion and spirituality are outmoded by the impressive
explanatory powers of positivistic science; no longer so sure
that psychic phenomena (seemingly contradictory to materialistic science) are explained away as deception, error, and
fraud; no longer so sure that the search for a Universal moral
order is fruitless.

In simplest terms, the historical development of modern
science, because of its being an integral part of the long-
term multifold modernization trend, took on a particular bias.
Although *all* of our experience is "subjective" in the most
basic sense, science undertook to study exhaustively only
that portion which is our subjective experiencing of the data
of our physical senses -- meanwhile ignoring if not disparag-
ing that part of our subjective experience which has to do
with nonsensory, intuitive knowing. Initially this amounted
to a sort of "division of labor" vis-a-vis the church.

However, the methods of science became extremely powerful, as regards generating technologies for manipulating the physical universe. As a consequence their prestige led to an overshadowing of the inquiries of the humanities and religions into matters of value and meaning. Knowledge that could generate new technologies became that knowledge deemed of most worth, and the whole of science took on the prediction-and-control values of technology-focused knowledge.

This rise of materialistic science has been one of the most remarkable evolutionary leaps in the history of man. Its essence embodies a remarkable proposition, namely, that objective knowledge should not be based on religious or traditional authority, nor be the guarded property of an elite priesthood, but should be empirically based and publicly verifiable, open and free to all. It required, and obtained, consensus on the rules of validation. Thus we do not have (in general) Russian chemistry versus American chemistry, or Hindu astronomy versus Christian astronomy. Around the globe there is only science -- the best set of conceptual models and empirical relationships yet available, continuously tested in public by agreed-upon procedures.

Now we are approaching a similar development in the other half of human experience, wherein the rest of subjective experience becomes subject also to the same sort of open, free, publicly validated search for empirical truth. This new "noetic"* science would eliminate the apparent contradiction between the experiential understanding of Hindu, Moslem, and Christian. For the first time in history we see emerging a growing, progressively funded body of empirically established experience about man's inner life -- particularly about the perennial wisdom of the great religious traditions and gnostic groups. For the first time there is hope that this knowledge can become, not a secret repeatedly lost in dogmatization and institutionalization, or degenerating into manifold varieties of cultism and occultism, but the living heritage of all mankind.

---

*The root of the word "noetic" is the same as for the words gnosis, diagnosis, agnostic, and knowledge; it refers to intuitive knowing. William James used the term in *The Varieties of Religious Experience* in defining mysticism.

A Utopian Perspective on the Future

Response: William H. Garrison

Someone asked me what my credentials were in order to be responding to Dr. Harman; I was concerned about that until I heard him this morning. Looking around the crowd here, I don't see anybody who is qualified to respond to Dr. Harman -- so, it might as well be me. I suspect that the person who was scheduled originally to do this read the prepared material sent to him ahead of time and asked his wife please to reschedule her surgery for the week of December 11. So, here I am!

Having had the material in advance and having read it quite a few times, I would like to try to capsule what Dr. Harman has said to us. He indicated that he was an optimist among a great crowd of pessimists, and he has come to us and said that we are at the threshold of not only great change, but at the threshold of an *accelerating rate* of change.

I don't think any of us are prepared to disagree with him as to this. Rather, each one of us here senses we live in a time and generation in which the characteristic is change. But in his role as the optimist, he is suggesting to us the possibility of a new science, a science of what heretofore has been extrasensory perception, the science of the unconscious. In this new science remote viewing, precognition will be synthesized in the years to come with the traditions of the great religions, of which Christianity is only one, and including Islam, Hinduism, Buddhism, and others. Even the present preoccupation with the occult, the fascination with the cults, the extreme varieties of which have been brought to

our attention lately, he sees optimistically as being synthesized into a new awareness of the nonsensory realities.

As far as the *fact of* change itself is concerned, there is
no way by which any of us could disagree with him. But we
could take issue with him on his optimistic view. As a matter
of fact, he acknowledges that there are more pessimists in his
field than there are optimists.

But my role as a responder is not to take issue with him so
much as to try to highlight or sharpen the focus of the issue
as it relates to the church and whatever agenda it should develop for itself to meet this changing situation.

As a layman, I am constrained to say that one of the problems with the church developing an agenda is that it has had
such a difficult time down through the centuries in establishing what its own mission is.

Howard Snyder, writing in a symposium on the Lausanne Congress, said that Protestantism has never fully developed a
fully biblical doctrine of the church. He said our concept
of the church is one we inherited from the Catholic church,
where it was developed in the fourth century by Augustine,
and we have never given any real serious thought to what the
church is and what it ought to be. He states the only answer
to this is to "return to the Scriptures and self-consciously
to dig out a biblical ecclesiology that does not conflict with
biblical soteriology." And he has attempted to do that, I
think, in his latest book.

John Stott, in his book, *Christian Missions in the Modern
World,* says that the greatest need in current ecumenical debate is to find an agreed biblical hermeneutic, for without
this a broader consensus on the meaning and obligation of
missions is unlikely ever to be reached. The dilemma as I
see it, as a layman, is that you professionals, nineteen centuries after Jesus Christ declared that He was going to found
His church (Matthew 16), are not only undecided over the mission, but Dr. Stott says you need to understand how to interpret the Bible to discover that mission.

At the threshold of change as described by Dr. Harman, it
seems about time the church should decide what its mission is.
If I may venture my own opinion, it seems that down through
the years the church has been torn between attending to its
own institutional welfare and to the business of promoting
the spiritual welfare of its people. It seems to have rocked

between the extremes of sponsoring crusades to rescue the
Holy Land from the disciples of Mohammed to the extremely
pietistic movements which have been anti-organizational in
all respects.

And, as a layman, I would like to suggest that the business of the church is to produce men and women who are distinctive in their service to mankind and distinctive in their
witness for Jesus Christ. There are plenty of biblical models. We had a beautiful model presented to us last night
when our attention was focused on Noah. If I were picking a
model this morning, I would pick Daniel. Daniel is an excellent example of a man who lived his entire productive life in
a totally hostile environment, an environment which must have
been a frustration at every turn to the sensibilities of this
Jewish teen-ager who was taken to Babylon to live his entire
life. But he lived victoriously; he lived *against* the stream.
He prayed when it was *against* the law to pray. He prayed
openly, and he took the consequences of it. He was a man of
the Word; in Daniel 9 we find him reading the writings of
Jeremiah. He claimed the promises of God for his people, at
the same time confessing the sins of his people. He was a
man who lived significantly for God within the enormous tensions of his day. And I believe that because of the distinc-
tiveness of his lifestyle, the great ruler Nebuchadnezzar had
his conversion experience (as recorded in Daniel 4). The secular historians, of course, record nothing of any social
transformation which occurred in Babylon because of Nebuchadnezzar's conversion, but I am convinced that at that point in
time he became a man of God.

The business of the church, if you will, is to produce the
Daniels of our day, and there have been some. Last year I
had a delightful time in meeting and talking with Dr. Ralph
Winter. He called my attention to the work he has done in
the sodality-modality discussion, and pointed out so vividly
that many of the great improvement movements of the church
have resulted from men and emphases *outside* the mainstream of
the church. The business of the church is to produce the
peoples of God, to nurture them, to encourage them, and to
support them in whatever avenues God leads them to be distinctive servants in their respective days. So, because we
believe the church is supernatural -- or it administers God's
supernatural program for ministering to the needs of mankind
-- we have to take issue with Dr. Harman's utopian or optimistic view as he sees Christianity as only a part of a great
synthesis. Because we see it as totally unique, the *only*
"philosophy" that directs men to God as the solution to their

problems, we cannot see it becoming a part of such a synthesis as Dr. Harman envisions. All other religions and philosophies ultimately direct man back to himself and his own resources.

We must recognize the change. We must see that it is here. We must take comfort in the fact that Jesus declared *He* was going to build His church. The forces of hell will not prevail against it. It is exactly on schedule -- it is not one day early, not one day behind. This age will be consummated in His own time, and if we would be a part of the program of God, it is up to us to have understanding and perspective of what God is doing -- as Daniel did in his day and time -- and to live significantly, even as he did.

We can live with a sense of expectancy. I have always been fascinated by Moses, at 120 years of age, standing there on the east side of the Jordan river, looking at the Judean wilderness and getting excited and saying to God, "Thy servant has just begun to see what a great and mighty God can do." And he tried to prevail on God to let him go into the land to experience afresh what that great and mighty God was going to do.

I think that the church today -- in the light of the change about which Dr. Harman is talking -- had better be prepared to articulate its mission and to *come together on its mission.* I suggest that this mission is the nurturing, the building, the evangelizing of men and women to live for God; to give them a sense of expectancy that God is going to accomplish His plan and His purpose -- *and that we can be a part of it!* Particularly, we should expect the synthesis which Dr. Harman suggests is going to occur, but to the extent to which Christianity becomes a part of it and loses its distinctive and its exclusive emphasis upon directing men and women to the living God, it will become a syncretism -- a putting together of totally irreconcilable ideas.

We believe, with Dr. Harman, the change is coming. We had better be prepared to know what *God* is doing and *how we can serve Him* in our generation and in the generations to come!

Thank you.

A Dystopian Perspective on the Future: Challenge for the Churches

Address: Peter J. Henriot

I must be honest with you at the outset and say that I am very uncomfortable with the theme assigned me for my presentation here this afternoon, "A Dystopian Perspective on the Future." My discomfort is twofold. First, I'm not sure what the word "dystopia" means. It's a neologism, and when I looked for it in my dictionary, I couldn't find it. But, second, as the antithesis of "utopia," it seems to imply "pessimism." By personality, I am basically optimistic -- even though I frequently respond to people who ask me if I'm optimistic or pessimistic, that on Monday, Wednesday, and Friday I'm optimistic, and on Tuesday, Thursday, and Saturday I'm pessimistic -- and on Sunday I pray. Seriously, by professional training as a social scientist, I am wary of simplistic optimistic/pessimistic dichotomies.

Yet, uncomfortable as I may be, I still believe it is important to explore this perspective with you as you consult on "An Evangelical Agenda -- 1984 and Beyond." The perspective dramatically raises the challenge of change in our world today, change which offers both promises and problems. And the perspective situates the demanding task for any church that would be true to its mission today: how to present the "Good News" amidst so much "bad news."

Therefore, let me move beyond my uncomfortableness to offer you some thoughts for your own reflection and planning. I want briefly this afternoon to address: (1) the meaning of a "perspective," (2) the elements of this dystopian perspective, (3) some analysis related to this perspective, and (4) a few implications of such a perspective for the church.

MEANING OF PERSPECTIVE

We do not see reality head-on, eyes-open, unfocused. Our perceptions are set within a framework or perspective which highlights certain aspects and shades others. This framework or perspective, sometimes referred to as "mindset," is something like a pair of glasses. We see reality *through* these glasses. But where do we get these glasses, i.e., acquire this mindset or perspective? It is made up, at the deepest level, of the most basic assumptions, attitudes, and felt values held by the individual and promoted by the culture. It is something to which we are socialized, over the years of our experience of formal and nonformal education, communications, reflection, and social exchange.

Because the mindset which shapes, forms, and colors our perception of reality is so important, it needs to be continually examined and critically evaluated. We do that from time to time when we are sharply challenged, when we become aware that we are growing "out of touch," or when we feel called to more precise clarification of our position in the world.

A perspective can be a very broad outlook on reality, something which enables us to pull together a lot of data and systematically relate it. I would call such a perspective "holistic" -- giving a view of the whole -- and I believe that the dystopian perspective has just such a holistic character. A holistic perspective is made up of (1) elements and (2) analysis. The elements of a perspective are the various items, insights, or emphases which provide the basic data. The analysis is the intellectual ordering of this data, done in order to understand the relationships, linkages, among the elements. Analysis as such takes very seriously the *structures* of reality.

ELEMENTS OF PERSPECTIVE

What, then, can we say are the elements of a dystopian perspective? I suspect that all of you here this afternoon could answer this question very well if I simply asked you to take a sheet of paper and list the five most serious challenges facing our nation and globe before the end of the Twentieth Century. We have become used to dire predictions, disturbing descriptions, and distressing discussions of what is wrong today and what will be more wrong tomorrow. Perhaps we have

become too used to all of this, and what I have to say will
simply be repetitive of what you already know. Let's face
it: there is the danger of the "ho hum" in all this dystopia stuff.

But I wonder whether we really do know the seriousness of
the situation which faces us in the years ahead? Really, do
we know it well enough to recognize its implications for some
radical change in the way we look at things, or expect certain things to always happen, or allow a "business as usual"
approach toward moving into the future? Every age has been
filled with dangers, declines, disasters -- and doom-sayers.
It is frequently a clever way to put down those who would say,
"But *this time* it's really serious," by quoting something
from a classical author witnessing the fall of the Roman Em-
pire, or a medieval author lamenting the breakup of Christendom, or a Victorian author dreading the dawn of the Twentieth
Century. Yet, even at this risk of a putdown, I still will
say to you with some conviction and passion: "But this time
it *is* really serious!" There is not only a quantitative but
a qualitative dimension in the newness of the threat to human survival.

Let me outline the elements which I see, as a political
scientist engaged in policy analysis relating to global and
domestic social issues -- the elements which make up the dystopian perspective we need to grapple with. I've categorized
the five most serious challenges facing us before the end of
the Twentieth Century as the following: military, economic,
ecological, political, and cultural.

1. Military

It is an awesome and never-to-be-forgotten fact that we
constantly live under the "Sword of Damocles" of nuclear holocaust. Since 1945 we have grown increasingly capable of ob-
literating life on our planet. At this very moment, as we
sit here near a large metropolitan center, some of our brothers and sisters in other countries have nuclear missiles
pointed at us which, if launched as I speak, could -- before
our coffee break -- wipe us off the face of the globe fifteen
times over -- whatever it means to be wiped off fifteen times
over! And we similarly have missiles pointed at our brothers
and sisters which can wipe them off the face of the globe
fifteen times over. This "balance of terror" has been termed
"Mutually Assured Destruction" or -- and very appropriately
-- MAD.

Followed in the name of "national security," the MAD strategy has been compounded by the proliferation of present nuclear capability and future nuclear potential around the globe.
The United States, the Soviet Union, China, France, England,
and India now are nuclear powers; Israel, South Africa,
Brazil, and who knows who else will soon be nuclear powers.
By the end of this century, the possibility of some "irresponsible" agent -- be it nation, guerrilla band, criminal gang
-- using atomic weapons to threaten, harass, retaliate, or
simply push, is all too likely. And add to this the danger
of "accident" as more and more nuclear weaponry is stockpiled
in this country and around the globe. Even our most sophisticated technology is not accident-immune, as we know from
almost daily reports of aircraft near-misses or oil-tanker
spills. What makes us think -- hope -- that nuclear capability, proliferated at an increasingly rapid rate, will be
without accidental dangers even if not deliberately used for
destructive purposes? You are here to plan on an agenda for
"1984 and beyond." I am not   nor do I mean to be -- melo-
dramatic by stating that we will be lucky -- *blessed* -- to
reach 1984!

But even if we could avoid nuclear disaster, can nations
continue to escalate spending for armaments at the expense of
spending for social needs? The United Nations Special Session on Disarmament last Spring estimated that the combined
military budget of all countries -- First World, Second World,
Third World -- now exceeds over $400 billion a year! An un-
imaginable figure, but proportionately more than what is spent
on the needs of education, health, housing, agriculture, etc.

In our own country, we presently see a national budget promoted which trims social programs but increases military
spending. As someone has ironically remarked, we -- and the
citizens of the Soviet Union, of China, of numerous African
and Latin American and Asian states -- are in serious danger
of being a people richly defended but poorly educated, housed,
and cared for! Armaments, instruments of destruction, are
unacceptable wastes of our scarce resources of materials,
intelligence, finances, and will. And every projection indicates that, even with SALT II, military spending and all it
implies is on the increase around the world.

2. Economic

The second element of a dystopian perspective is one which
hardly needs considerable elaboration for this audience. You
yourselves daily experience the economic crisis in terms of

higher prices you must pay to meet the needs of the churches
or organizations you lead as well as those of the families
you belong to. Inflation in the United States is now "double
digit," hovering around the 10 percent mark. And studies
show that inflation hits hardest at the basics -- food, energy, shelter, medicine -- and hence hits hardest at the poor
and lower-income people. Unemployment is officially around
5.8 percent, the lowest in recent years. Yet since that figure only indicates those who are continuing to search for a
job -- and does not include those so discouraged that they
have quit looking -- the unofficial national figure is probably closer to 9-10 percent. The figure for nonwhite unemployment is around 12 percent; for youth, around 16-18 percent; for nonwhite youth, between 35-40 percent.

During the past several months -- as the dollar has fluc-
tuated on the world market -- more and more public officials
have spoken of the possibility of a new recession; some even
speak privately of the fear of a *depression*. You've probably
heard the joke that says we have a recession when my next-door
neighbor loses his job, and a depression when I lose my job.
But the domestic economic crisis is no joke! With the increasing uncertainty of adequate energy available to maintain
our present styles and modes of industrial growth, with the
cities -- especially in the North -- decaying in housing
stock and public services, and with the generation of a new
urban underclass -- or marginated men and women -- we have
serious problems.

Our domestic economic problems are situated, of course,
within a global economic crisis. Inflation is a worldwide
disease, affecting industrialized and developing countries
alike. But it is particularly true in the developing countries, the so-called "Third World" of Latin America, Asia,
and Africa, where the economic reality is the cruelest.
Robert McNamara, president of the World Bank, estimates that
today over 800 million people -- one-fifth of the globe's
population -- live in what has been termed *absolute poverty*:
"a condition of life so characterized by malnutrition, illiteracy, disease, squalid surroundings, high infant mortality,
and low life expectancy as to be beneath a reasonable definition of human decency." The World Bank projects only a modest decline in these figures for the year 2000, and that only
if some significant structural changes were made in the patterns of North/South relationships, e.g., trade, commodity
prices, aid, monetary relationships, investments, and power.
These structural changes -- many of them embodied in the poor
countries' call for a New International Economic Order

(NIEO) -- would, of course, have profound implications for
the U. S. economic system and standard of living.

A depressing -- indeed, dystopian -- fact is that the gap
between rich and poor countries, the North/South cleavage, is
widening. As Aurelio Peccei, head of the Club of Rome, remarked just recently, this cleavage

> ... divides the world even more drastically than the
> ideological and political walls which separate East and
> West; and, short of radical measures, it will prove un-
> bridgeable. Commanding 80% of the world's wealth and
> trade, over 90% of the industry and services, and
> nearly 100% of the institutions of research, the human
> groups of the North have grown to such gigantic dimen-
> sions that they can dominate the world by sheer weight.

The problems of the Third World have a terrible relationship to the military element of the dystopian perspective.
In a recent Rand Corporation study prepared for the United
States Air Force, Guy J. Pauker foresees a growing conflict
between the Third World and the rich world. He doubts that
we in the U.S. are ready to yield our accumulated wealth and
privilege or to negotiate with the Third World from other
than a position of strength. The Rand study further suggests
that existing mechanisms of global planning and management
are incapable of handling the upheaval caused by population
growth, strain on resources, damage to the environment, and
obsolete patterns of administration and decision making.
Pauker envisions riots, mass migrations, water diversions,
poaching in coastal zones, and deep-sea grabs. His suggestion is that the United States should be able to respond
militarily to these threats.

3. Ecological

I read with great interest the report of this group's
Atlanta Consultation last December. The introductory overview by Donald Hoke reviewed the recent reports of the Club
of Rome, projections of a situation called the "global prob-
lematique" to specify five major trends of global concern:
accelerating industrialization, rapid population growth,
widespread malnutrition, depletion of nonrenewable resources,
and a deteriorating environment. I am a member of the U. S.
Association for the Club of Rome, a group of one-hundred-plus
men and women who feel that the messages -- both optimistic
and pessimistic -- of the Club of Rome should be given wider
attention by citizens and policy makers alike in this country.

What disturbs me is the backlash which frequently results
when the distressing news is made public that the resources
of our globe are finite.

The "ecological imperative" of finding a balance between
human endeavors and the natural environment -- a balance that
is socially just as well as physically sustainable -- is no
easy task. That it is a task which will not go away will be
evidenced in the soon-to-be-released U.S. government report
entitled, *Global 2000*, a report requested by President Carter
of the Council on Environmental Quality in order to present
to the U.S. public the latest projections on the probable
changes in the world's population, natural resources, and environment through the end of this century. I served as an
advisor in the preparation of this report, and I know, from
reading and debating its earlier drafts, that *Global 2000*
will present a grim picture. While the developing countries
press the earth's carrying capacity with increasing population, the industrialized countries do even greater harm, in
my opinion, by wasting the earth's resources with affluent,
needless consumption.

The most serious challenge in the ecological element of
this dystopian perspective is that delays in responding to
the developing crises bring about even greater problems. We
simply cannot keep postponing greater conservation of scarce
fossil-fuel resources, postponing creation and utilization of
solar energy and other renewable resources, postponing curbs
on water, air, and land pollution, postponing a population
policy that recognizes people have smaller families only when
their general standard of living is improving. We cannot
postpone these steps, that is, if we hope to survive.

Lester Brown has recently published a study entitled, *The
Twenty Ninth Day*, describing the dangers to the earth's biological systems. His title emphasizes the urgency for action
by recalling a French riddle used to teach children the meaning of exponential growth. A lily pond, the riddle goes,
contains a single leaf. Each day the number of leaves dou-
bles -- two leaves the second day, four the third, eight the
fourth, and so on. Question: If the pond is completely full
on the thirtieth day, when is it half-full? Answer: On the
twenty-ninth day. In relating to many aspects of the global
ecological scene, today we are at the twenty-ninth day.

4. Political

I am a political scientist, and though I believe, along
with thinkers as diverse as Aristotle and Karl Marx, that
economics is a basic structure of our human society, I am
particularly partial to the importance of the political category. Constructing a dystopian perspective, then, I would
emphasize here some very distressing trends in the political
element.

The first trend is the decline of democracy. By this I
do not mean simply the "forms" of democracy (popular vote,
representative assemblies, etc.), but even more the "substance" (decisions made for the benefit of the common good)
and the "spirit" (commitment to a common search for the promotion of full human rights). Just last Sunday, December 10,
we celebrated the thirtieth anniversary of the Universal Declaration of Human Rights. This great and important United
Nations document reminds us that human rights are civil-
political (free press, fair trial, etc.) and also social-
economic (employment, education, etc.). Countries of whatever system -- socialist, capitalist, communist, mixed --
which do not promote full human rights for the benefit of all
their people are nondemocratic, whatever they may claim to
be. The United States has been blessed with years of democracy. But the danger of complacency -- marked by a failure
to vote responsibly, a reluctance to criticize serious de-
fects, a rise in "respectable fraud" -- should push us to
examine the state of our blessings a little more closely,
especially as it involves the socio-economic rights of all
our people.

The second trend is the rise of authoritarian regimes, the
so-called "national security states." One does not need to
look only at the obvious abuses in the Soviet Union, China,
or other communist states. For in the name of "fighting communism," many Latin American military dictatorships -- some
of them sadly, in my opinion, supported by our own U.S. government -- suppress any efforts at land reform, improved working conditions or more just distribution of income. African
states of the left and of the right stifle participation in
the name of "stability." And even in the older democracies
of the West, unrest caused by economic problems is sometimes
met with more police to maintain the status quo rather than
more efforts to improve the situation.

A third trend is the use of new methods of control of people, such as technological surveillance and increasingly

sophisticated spying. We have been sufficiently shocked in
recent years by revelations in our country concerning our
FBI and CIA to know that this trend is indeed politically
dangerous.

The fourth trend, however, is one which I find particularly distressing. It is a theoretical critique and a practical response by the "neo-conservatives." These are not the
old cranky conservatives who were against, in principle, every
political effort to improve socio-economic conditions. No,
these are a new brand, whom I refer to as "hand wringing
conservatives." They admit that there are terrible problems,
much hunger, awful torture, horrible suffering (as they wring
their hands). But it really isn't possible to make much of
a change, that's the way things always are, people's expectations are too high, "the poor we have always with us," and
any effort to change things will just make matters worse --
all these things said usually by people who aren't hungry,
aren't being tortured, aren't suffering.

5. Cultural

Finally, a few remarks about the cultural element in a
dystopian perspective. Surely one of the most destructive
trends of recent years has been the rise of an exaggerated
individualism represented by the mentality of: "Do your own
thing," "Look out for Number One," "Get yours before somebody
else does," "If I worked for it, it's mine," and -- most de-
pressingly -- "God takes care of them that takes care of
themselves!" This individualism gets reinforced in a
consumption-oriented society. Advertising techniques emphasize how much (i.e., how many *things*) each of us must have
for our own personal use if we are to be truly happy. Politically this shows up in a spirit of competition, aggression,
and lack of care and respect for others -- especially if
they are nonproductive people like the elderly, retarded,
women, etc.

Culturally, we still struggle mightily in this country (to
speak only about the U.S.) with racism, sexism, and classism.
Poor people are looked down upon and often made to feel
guilty. Women are considered second-class, and their struggle
for equality ridiculed or called pushy or unnatural when what
we -- men in positions of influence -- usually mean is that
it is challenging our power. And tensions between whites and
nonwhites remain as we continue to work out the consequences
of a heritage of being a nation which in our founding spoke
of equality in the Declaration of Independence but institu-

tionalized slavery in our Constitution. Surely a particularly distressing element in a dystopian perspective is how
we can still come to meetings to plan for the future and
yet be without many people of lower income, many women, or
many nonwhites.

Perhaps one of the most serious cultural threats today
is the rise of the "lifeboat" and "triage" theories to ab-
solve those of us in more fortunate circumstances from taking steps and making the sacrifices necessary to meet the
needs of our less fortunate brothers and sisters in this
country and around the world. This point was eloquently
touched on during last year's Consultation in the address of
David McKenna. I would only add a footnote to emphasize the
seriousness of the destructive threat to fully human survival posed by this kind of thinking. The eminent English
scientist-philosopher, Lord C. P. Snow, was asked several
years ago what he thought would be the most terrible thing
that could happen to us in the years ahead. That millions
of people would die of starvation? No, he said, not that
millions of people would die of starvation, but that millions
would die of starvation *and* we would watch them die on col-
ored television. Because then we would die, too! What does
it mean -- in terms of basic human survival, in any cultural
sense of human civilization -- if some few live at the needless, and I emphasize *needless*, expense of many others?

ANALYSIS OF PERSPECTIVE

Having listed the military, economic, ecological, political, and cultural elements which might go into making up a
dystopian perspective, I now want to turn to some analysis.
As I mentioned at the outset, a perspective includes an analysis, whether it be explicit or implicit. Analysis is the
intellectual ordering of the relationships, the linkages,
among the various elements; it points out what social scientists call the structural connections. In order to grapple
with this dystopian perspective in an adequate and creative
fashion, I believe that we must move from the anecdotal to
the analytical, move from stories about the problems to seeing their structural linkages and interdependencies.

There are obviously many analyses which could be drawn on
at this point. From my own training and background, I choose
a structural approach from "political economy." I have found
it helpful to look at the present crisis -- in both its domestic and global dimensions -- in terms of an analytical description set forth by a colleague of mine at the Center of

Concern, Joe Holland. This analytical description outlines
three major stages of industrialization and situates the current crisis -- marked by the various elements described in
the dystopian perspective -- within the third stage of industrialization.

The first or early stage of industrialization was characterized by a frequently ruthless laissez-faire capitalism.
(Think for a moment of the novels of Charles Dickens and his
description of working conditions and their impact on the
lives of the poor.) In the late nineteenth and early twentieth centuries, this stage was in the industrialized *center*
(mainly the North Atlantic powers), marked by a primitive,
labor-intensive technology, gross labor exploitation, a non-
regulatory state, and minimal social services. In the colon-
ial *periphery* (the so-called "underdeveloped world"), this
stage was marked by a plunder of cheap raw materials and a
limited market for finished goods.

The second or middle stage of industrialization, especially in the period preceding and following the Second World
War, has been referred to as corporate, social-welfare capitalism. In the industrial center, this stage meant a more
advanced technology with labor/capital balance, strong
workers' movements (unionization), a moderately regulatory
state, and benevolent social policies (e.g., the era of the
New Deal). In the neo-colonial periphery of the "emerging
nations," linkages to the rich nations continued to be
forged; in addition to supplying raw materials, these nations
now served as new bases for more labor-intensive industrial
operations in an international division of labor and also
provided enlarged markets for finished goods.

A third stage, late industrialization, is the most recent
and is only now beginning. This is the stage of transnational
capitalism -- a new form of laissez-faire capitalism because
uncontrolled by any transnational regulation. Since it is
just beginning, we can only intuit at the present some future
lines of development. Under the impetus of highly efficient
and competitive multinational corporations, the process of
industrialization is moving toward becoming worldwide, international competition becomes the dominant economic fact, and
national life is more and more organized around "efficiency"
in international competition. (Think, for example, of the
recent conflicts in this country over imports of textiles,
electronics, steel, and automobiles.) The nation-state becomes to the global market what the corporation was to the
domestic market.

In this third stage appear many of the dystopian elements
mentioned earlier in this paper. Rich and poor countries
will become more interdependent, drawn together by the forces
of transnational capitalism. They may also become tragically
closer in common sufferings, at least for many of the less
fortunate. Because of a great reliance on a highly central-
ized, capital-intensive, and automated-cybernetic style,
large percentages of the human family, in both the center
and the periphery, are marginalized as there is a tendency
toward high unemployment (especially among minorities), spi-
raling inflation, curtailed social services, and harassment
or repression of opposition, especially of organized labor.
The "National Security State" -- with attendant violation of
human rights -- is a natural outcome of this situation. Ecological considerations are disregarded, whether in the strip-
mining of Appalachia, or the building of nuclear reactors in
Brazil, or the offshore drilling in the North Sea.

What I hope to do by this brief exposition of one analysis
which fits into a dystopian perspective is suggest the "radical" -- in the sense of "root" -- character of the challenge
before us. Willis Harman has spoken of the social and historical forces which are gathering to bring about a great
transformation of industrialized society. This utopian perspective is indeed exciting. But there is also the dystopian
perspective that suggests that there are severe structural
obstacles to this transformation. We have to take these
obstacles seriously. For example, we might want to explore
further the serious problems posed by the economic and political force which large multinational corporations exercise
today and the ecological and cultural consequences of the
corporate style of operation.

IMPLICATIONS OF PERSPECTIVE

It seems to me that the dystopian perspective does indeed
have critical implications for the church, and for any "Evangelical Agenda -- 1984 and Beyond." As I understand the program of this Consultation, you will be addressing some of
these implications in the following sessions. Let me at
least outline some of the questions which I would suggest
flow from the perspective I have presented. For I believe
that the dystopian elements and analysis offer a strong challenge to the future agenda -- indeed for the future *being* --
of the church.

Let me say at this point that I do not offer these suggestions as a totally neutral observer, as simply a value-free

social scientist. I have presented to you this afternoon the
results of the study, reflection, and experience of a professional political scientist who has been for seven years engaged in policy research, advocacy, and education on issues
of global development -- the work I do at the Center of Concern in Washington, D. C. My values, however, are heavily
influenced by two important facts: The first is the year I
spent in Latin America, 1976-1977, living and working for
most of the time amidst the wretchedly poor of a squatters'
barrio in Medellin, Colombia. These were people for whom a
dystopian perspective is a present, not a future, reality,
and their condition deeply touched my life and vocation. I
will always read the data of today through their eyes. The
second fact is that, in addition to being a political scientist, I am a Christian, have a master's degree in theology,
am an ordained Roman Catholic priest, and a member of the
Jesuit Order. My concern for the church is personal and
deep, growing out of a love for Jesus Christ and for His
people, my brothers and sisters. And so I hope that I offer
these suggestions and questions as one who stands with you
in a common quest for evangelical, Gospel concerns.

I believe that the basic question the church must ask itself is how tied it is -- in attitudes and behavior -- to
some of the present structures which underlie the dystopian
situation I have sketched. By that I mean that a serious ex-
amination of the message you preach, of the values you foster,
of the lifestyle you follow, of the future you envision, must
be a central task for any continuing consultation. For example, what kind of word does the church speak about armaments and the madness of the nuclear race? What is the relation of the church to the economic structures which domesti-
cally and globally seem so incapable of meeting the basic
human needs of the poor majority of the people? What lifestyle characterizes the leaders of the church in a time of
resource scarcity and environmental deterioration? What is
the "political stance" of the church in the face of declining
democracy, rising authoritarianism, and a debilitating "neo-
conservatism"? (Obviously, the church cannot be politically
neutral; not to take a stance *is* to take a stance.) And what
is the impact of the church culturally in terms of racism,
sexism, classism? In a third stage of industrialization,
what is the role of a church which because of its universal
mandate must itself be transnational?

To repeat the basic question, how tied is the church to
the present structures which underlie the dystopian situation? Only if it comes to grips with this question -- and

the consequences of honest answers -- can it hope to be able
to offer a counter-perspective to the dystopian perspective
I have spoken of. Such a counter-perspective is truly needed,
I believe, and it would emphasize three things: vision,
values, and vocation.

First, the *vision* needs to be a product of people who can
"dream dreams." The English economist who has so strongly
influenced the new generation of dreamers, E. F. Schumacher,
wrote not long before his death last year, "Western industrialized society is rich in means and poor in ends." We need
reasons -- ends -- for doing what we do. An evangelical
church has plenty of reasons to draw on. But are they presented in a vision which motivates, a vision which is relevant to today in the sense of speaking to the military, economic, ecological, political, and cultural crises?

Second, the *values* need to be clearly counter to the values foisted on us by modern communications. I frequently
suggest to audiences that if they want to know about the dominant values of the United States, read *Newsweek* and *Time*.
But don't read the articles, read the advertisements. These
show all too graphically the values that need to be countered.
And, in my opinion, an evangelical agenda needs to be concerned not so much with the anti-woman view of sex offered
by the ads (bad as it is), as with the economic system geared
for wasteful production which must use this view of sex in
order to promote affluent consumption.

Third, the *vocation* needs to make manifest the call to
serve in a world where increasingly that service requires
sacrifice because it means service of the poor, in terms not
of charity but of justice. It is a vocation based on the
recognition that our humanity is ultimately shaped by our
decisions for justice. And that has a lot to do with our
faith. I believe I have solid theological grounds for that
assertion. For me it rests upon a biblical understanding of
vocation. Among the many texts I might cite, I simply remind
ourselves here that the test -- the only test -- for entry
into the Kingdom of God is given by Jesus in the 25th chapter of Matthew. Today we know very clearly that feeding the
hungry, housing the homeless, comforting the sick, visiting
the imprisoned, are not merely acts of charity we are bound
to perform. They are also works of justice, which have structural implications in the social, political, economic, and
cultural life of our nation and globe.

There is need, then, for a perspective which offers vision, values, and vocation. This is a need for something radically counter to the dystopian perspective I have offered here. But it is not, I believe, a need for a utopian perspective. It is a need for an *evangelical perspective* -- one which engenders a commitment, a lifestyle, which is truly "counter cultural."

CONCLUSION

In conclusion, I return to my opening remarks about my being an optimist on Monday, Wednesday, and Friday, a pessimist on Tuesday, Thursday, and Saturday -- while I pray on Sunday. Well, this has been Tuesday, and you have heard my pessimistic, dystopian perspective. But I am in the midst of a group of men and women for whom *every day* is Sunday. And so, if I may be permitted a concluding moment of personal testimony or witness as a fellow-Christian: for me there is ultimately neither utopia nor dystopia. There is only the Kingdom of God, proclaimed in the life, death, and resurrection of Jesus. This Kingdom has meaning for today, in the lives of our brothers and sisters around us close at hand and throughout our globe. To make it real -- and not alienating rhetoric -- in the social, economic, political, and cultural structures of our lives, is *the* challenging "Evangelical Agenda -- for 1984 and Beyond!"

A Dystopian Perspective on the Future: Challenge for the Churches

Response: David E. Johnston

Twice in his address, Dr. Henriot asked the question:
"To what extent is the church tied to the present structures
which underlie the dystopian situation?" In the hope of providing some grist for the further discussion which we will
have today in our groups, I would like to raise questions
which deal with the specific areas of concern discussed by
Dr. Henriot. These questions relate to our role as evangelicals and concern our own ties to these specific structures.

As you remember, Dr. Henriot discussed five structures:
military, economic, ecological, political, and cultural.

First, let's look at the *military*. What is our responsibility as Christians concerning the tremendous growth in
armaments in our own country and the other major powers in
the world? We do have the great hope, as Christians, of
Christ's return. Therefore, He will preserve the earth and
us for His return. But I wonder to what extent we, as evangelicals, should be the instruments He will use to preserve
the world for His return.

Turning to the *economic* side, what is the responsibility
of the largely middle-class evangelicals to the one-fifth of
the world's population without adequate food or to the needy
of our own society? Having grown up in evangelical churches,
listening to the messages of my own father, I have been reminded often of my responsibility to be a steward, especially to the local church. However, as Dr. Henriot has reminded us, in the text of Matthew 25, we are called to a

stewardship *beyond* giving to our local church building programs. How do we meet this responsibility to the underdeveloped areas of our own society and of the world? Compassionate alms-giving certainly will not solve the problems;
even radical redistribution of wealth will not provide long-
term solutions. But we evangelicals may have something to
say regarding models of economic development. As was mentioned this morning, we must have a response to the question,
"Is economic development the *primary* need?"

In the area of *ecology* and the preservation of natural resources, what do we have to say about the significant investment in facilities used only a few hours each week which is
typical of our suburban churches? What about the faith missions and evangelical ministries that require major commitments to resource gathering through fund-raising efforts?
Missionaries must devote considerable proportions of their
time in fund-raising efforts for their own support and that
of their sending agencies. What do we say about our own ac-
quisitiveness and that of other evangelicals with whom we
fellowship?

In the *political* arena, how will the church respond to
the growing trend toward authoritarianism in government?
Will we seek accommodation? Will we accept the liberation
theologies that are sometimes expounded today? What are our
responsibilities in the investment of our resources in individual companies? I recently met with a student who had
been active in the movement at the University of Minnesota
to ask that university to sell all its holdings in common
stock in companies involved in South Africa. Truly, this
is a complex issue, but should the only people addressing
the issue be universities that are secular?

The fifth structure in which Dr. Henriot found a dystopian trend is our *culture*. To what extent does our cultural
framework affect our concept of the outworking of the church?
Do we have a temptation to impose our own models of management and leadership in Third World areas where we work? In
our models of counseling and psychology, do we avoid the
trap of humanism? Surely, we are made in the image of God,
but it does not follow that the chief end of man is to glo-
rify himself.

Dr. Henriot concluded with the call for a *vision*. He
pointed out Dr. Schumacher's concern for simplicity and
urged us to develop our own "evangelical" vision. However,
he did not provide for us an *adequate* vision. We, as evan-

gelicals, have tended to be pessimistic. Scripture supports
our presumption that the world will not get better and that
evil will not be overcome completely until Christ returns
and Satan is finally restrained forever. Nevertheless, in
the face of our own dystopian predilections, our vision must
relate to our *primary responsibility* -- the propagation of
the Gospel. Included in that vision must be our responsibility to teach all that Christ commanded us and the mani-
festation of the work of the Holy Spirit in our own lives.

The Future of the Church: Its Nurture, Form, and Function

Address: Gene A. Getz

The purpose of this paper is to attempt to project the future of the church -- how it will carry on its functions and what forms and structures it will eventually take.

To facilitate your interaction with my observations, analyses, and projections in this presentation, it is important at the outset to present some of my basic definitions and assumptions.

DEFINITIONS AND ASSUMPTIONS

First, it is impossible to project the future of "the church" and its functions and forms without dealing with specific, localized bodies of believers. Therefore, I will hereafter use the term "church" to refer to "local churches" -- not the "universal church."

Second, there is little biblical data that can be brought to bear upon the actual future of "local churches" in our contemporary setting, except to say that the New Testament clearly illustrates for us that over a period of time first-century churches were at all levels of maturity. Furthermore, some were growing spiritually; others were stagnant; and some eventually deteriorated and actually ceased to exist. Simply stated, New Testament history and subsequent history reveals that local churches were not static in the area of maturity; rather they were in a constant state of change. It should not surprise us then, that we can observe the same process in the twentieth-century world.

Third, the Bible *does*, on the other hand, give us a wealth of data by which we can measure twentieth-century church life. It also gives us numerous principles which, if correctly applied, will help us produce mature churches.

Fourth, and closely related to the above, the Bible does not prescribe absolute forms, patterns, structures, or methodologies for church function. These are cultural dimensions of the church. This can be aptly demonstrated when we realize there is no church form ever completely spelled out or described in the New Testament. Furthermore, methods and approaches vary from one biblical setting to another. It is inappropriate, therefore, to absolutize a form or structure that is incomplete, or to fixate on methodology that is constantly varied in holy writ.

The term "principles," therefore, will be used to describe those aspects of the church considered to be normative and enduring from New Testament days until the present time. These principles emerge from normative directives given to New Testament churches and exemplary New Testament church functions and practices.

On the other hand, the terms "forms," "patterns," "structures," and "methods" will be used most often (usually synonymously) to refer to the cultural and changing aspects of the church. They simply represent the "means" that Christians are free to develop at any moment in history and in any given geographical setting in order to reach scriptural "ends." The important question is whether or not these "means" are in harmony with New Testament principles.

Fifth, scriptural writers often describe "functions" without describing "form" -- at least in detail. But in actual practice, there was always form. Wherever you have people, you have function. And wherever you have function, you have form. In other words, it is impossible to have a functioning "organism" without commensurate organization.

That biblical writers often described function without describing form is, I believe, by supernatural design. Had the Holy Spirit inspired descriptive methodology that is absolute, Christianity would have been "locked in" to a first-century, Middle-Eastern culture.

Some Bible interpreters tend to miss this unique and distinctive aspect in the Christian religion -- in reality a uniqueness that sets it off from most other world religions.

Because of our subjectivities, our insecurities, our limited
perspectives, and the inevitable influences of this world's
values and ways of doing things, we tend to superimpose
twentieth-century cultural norms and forms upon scriptural
functions.

When Dr. Kenneth Kantzer was interviewed this year relative to his new position as editor for *Christianity Today*,
he alluded to this problem when he was asked to give his opinion on the "major issues that evangelicals will have to deal
with in the next five years." Among other things, he stated
that one of these issues would be "the Americanization of the
church ... Evangelicals," he responded, "jeopardize their
biblical and traditional values by the infiltration of the
ideals of society."[1]

Sixth, a study of societies and groups reveals that people
usually do not change their ways of doing things apart from
various crises. We tend to fixate methodologically. People
generally become comfortable and secure in certain kinds of
social structures and usually will not change those structures without some kind of discomforting impetus.

This observation is particularly relevant to evangelical
Christians and is quite obvious in church history. Fixating
and absolutizing form and patterns is a natural tendency for
all people -- Christians and non-Christians. But it is even
more of a natural tendency for people who believe in eternal
and never-changing truth -- as evangelical Christians do.
Since it is very easy to confuse patterns and principles,
and since we all tend to develop security in form and structure, it is very easy for us to fall into the error of allow-
ing non-absolutes to become absolute, to confuse cultural
tradition with supra-cultural truth. This misunderstanding,
combined with our tendency to rationalize, forms a strong
deterrent to positive and necessary change.

A *seventh* assumption in this paper is that wherever there
are general trends, moods, crises, and struggles in our society and culture at large, there's always a "spillover" into
the subcultures of the world. This is probably best illustrated today by the women's rights issues, our open and con-
troversial discussions regarding homosexuality, and the varying questions and actual attacks on the traditional marital
and family value systems and structures.

Evangelicals, who, broadly defined, are a subculture within a larger culture, are face to face with these issues as

never before. The "spillover" is obvious. We have been driven, through change and subsequent crises, to face these issues head-on, attempting to arrive at a clear-cut biblical and theological perspective. It is my personal opinion that some of us are not faring too well in resolving these issues. Could it be that some evangelicals are so intent on keeping the basis of their faith respectable in the eyes of the world that they have opted for an errant Bible in order to achieve this goal?

This leads me to a *final* assumption. I am firmly committed to an inerrant Scripture. In projecting the forms and structures the church of the future will take, this is indeed a basic consideration, for those who depart from this basic presupposition will allow themselves liberties far beyond those of us who hold to a high view of inspiration of the Scriptures.

RESEARCH METHODOLOGY

An attempt to project the future of the church with any degree of accuracy is a rather awesome task. Obviously, I must approach the subject with a sense of "tentativeness" and with full awareness of my human and time limitations. However, in preparation for this presentation, I attempted to develop a research design that would help me arrive at a fairly accurate understanding of the immediate past as well as the ongoing present, particularly as it pertains to the forms and functions of the church. It is then, from this perspective, that I attempt to project the future.

First, I have naturally leaned heavily upon my academic and practical experience as a professor in preparing people for local church ministries.

Second, I have relied upon my biblical, historical, and cultural research in the area of ecclesiology, particulaly while a full-time professor at Dallas Theological Seminary, and which resulted in my book, *Sharpening the Focus of the Church*, published in 1974. Those of you who are familiar with my recent publications will recognize the results of this research in my definitions and assumptions. I'm committed to the idea that we cannot develop an adequate philosophy of the ministry leading to adequate strategies in the twentieth century without a total perspective. This perspective can only be kept in sharp and clear focus as we, on an ongoing basis, view our task through three lenses --

the lens₂of Scripture, the lens of history, and the lens of culture.

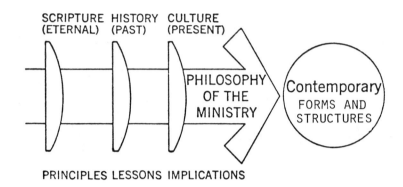

Third, I have gleaned a great deal from my practical experience over the last six years in helping plant Fellowship Bible church in Dallas and six branch churches. It is in this context I have attempted to apply creatively and in a renewal setting the principles I present in *Sharpening the Focus of the Church.*

Fourth, I have drawn on my continual research in practical areas of church life, as I have taught various concepts to these various congregations in Dallas. These concepts are most often reflected in my books entitled, *The Measure of a Man, The Measure of a Church, The Measure of a Family, The Measure of a Woman,* and *Building up One Another.*

Fifth, I have attempted to review most of the significant books written on the subject of the church in the last several years.

Sixth, to get a rather clear perspective on current trends and issues, I have reviewed rather carefully all relevant and significant articles written in five Christian periodicals over the last year -- *Christianity Today, Eternity, Christian Life, Moody Monthly,* and *Church Growth: America.*

Finally, I have arrived at some rather specific convictions based upon my experience in conducting various Church Renewal conferences, particularly in the last several years, in various seminaries, Bible colleges, denominational meetings, Christian Education conventions, and in local churches. All of these have been very helpful in assisting me to form some opinions regarding what professors, students, pastors, and other church leaders are feeling and sensing about the church as they engage in their various academic pursuits and practical ministries.

It is on the basis of these definitions and assumptions and within my own experiential context that I would like to rather succinctly present a profile of the church as I see the immediate past and the present, and then to project what I believe will be some future directions of the church, particularly as it relates to its nurture, its forms, and its functions.

THE PAST TO THE PRESENT

What has transpired in evangelical churches over the last several years is not unrelated to what has happened in our culture at large. During the late sixties and the early seventies, America began to experience an anti-institutional mood that actually threatened the very foundations of our society. It was during these years that students everywhere were rebelling.

These cultural upheavals and crises indeed "spilled over" into our evangelical subcultures. Most of us who were teaching on Christian campuses during those days remember fullwell the threatening questions and attacks on the various institutions in which we were teaching as well as their negative attitudes toward the institutional church.

A number of educators, theologians, and churchmen began to sincerely face these questions and to attempt to unravel the problem and sort out what was indeed valid in these reactions and what was simply unhappiness, frustration, and disillusionment caused by a society in crisis.

What was transpiring then in culture generally and in the evangelical subculture particularly also had significant historical roots. No crisis is ever precipitated in a vacuum. In the secular world, the "sacred cow" of science and its promised results were not working. There were no signs of the "great society." Furthermore, the adult world was in the

process of changing its moral value systems. More and more
youth were becoming very dissatisfied and disillusioned with
what they felt was a depersonalized society that was swallow-
ing them up, squelching their individuality, and destroying
their creative urges. They felt lost in a huge cultural
machine that was running out of control. They felt let down.
Their main recourse was to vent their anger on the institutions of America.

Intricately interwoven with these institutions in America
stood the churches and the Christian schools. The negative
"spillover" was immediate. But there were reasons. Christian institutions, too, appeared to many to be void of meaning and reality. To many, Christianity seemed merely academic and cognative, many times legalistic, and often superficial and unreal. Christianity, in its present form, seemed
to lack acceptable solutions for the big issues of the day.
In some instances we were not even talking about these issues.

The Church Renewal Movement

It was in those days that church renewal writers began to
speak to these issues. In the early sixties Elton Trueblood
published *The Company of the Committed*. Quoting Karl Heim in
his book, *Christian Faith and Natural Science*, he saw the
church as

> ... a ship on whose deck the festivities are still kept
> up and glorious music is heard, while deep below the
> waterline a leak has been sprung and masses of water
> are pouring in, so that the vessel is settling hourly
> lower though the pumps are manned day and night.

Findley Edge, a well-known spokesman and author in the
Southern Baptist convention, and a professor at the Louis-
ville seminary, picked up the same theme as Trueblood a
couple of years later. Experiencing disillusionment himself,
particularly over the continual growth in his own denomination and yet what he felt was the lack of Christian reality,
he wrote *A Quest for Vitality in Religion*. He wrote:

> At the present time churches are experiencing a period
> of almost unparalleled popularity and prosperity. Such
> a situation normally would be the base for unrestrained
> optimism and rejoicing. Strangely, such is not the
> case. Many thoughtful religious leaders and mature
> Christian laymen evidenced a growing ferment of uneasi-
> ness and concern. In spite of plush church buildings,

growing membership, and many vigorous activities that
are carried on within the churches, something is seriously wrong with modern Christianity. Something is
wrong at its center. It is in danger of losing its
life and dynamic.[4]

A few years later the spectrum of concern broadened when
a group of Christian educators representing various Christian schools met at Wheaton College's Honey Rock camp during
successive summers in 1967 and 1968. The result was Larry
Richards' *A New Face for the Church*, representing the thinking of the Honey Rock group generally, and his own thinking
particularly.

To most the book was radical. It called for a complete
evaluation and overhaul of our present church forms and structures, and, if necessary, to begin anew. But it was a stim-
ulating book. For many of us it did exactly what Richards
had hoped. In his foreword he wrote: "I also hope to stim-
ulate many to debate -- for in debating we conservatives are
driven back to Scripture to discover God's truth."[5]

A second book that appeared the same year was written by
Dr. Francis Schaeffer and entitled, *The Church at the End of
the Twentieth Century*. Writing out of a rather comprehensive
understanding of history and culture, he spoke directly to
the problem of differentiating absolutes from non-absolutes
in Scripture. "In a rapidly changing age like ours," he
wrote, "an age of total upheaval like ours, to make non-
absolutes absolute guarantees both isolation and the death
of the institutional, organized church."[6]

Also, beginning in 1970, we began to hear another very
significant American voice speaking from the Latin culture.
Howard A. Snyder, a missionary stationed in Sao Paulo,
Brazil, began to submit articles to various American maga-
zines. The titles themselves focused his concerns: "The
Fellowship of the Holy Spirit," published in *Christianity
Today*; "Church Renewal Through Small Groups," published in
United Evangelical Action;[8] "Does the Church Suffer an Edifice
Complex?" published in *World Vision*;[9] "'The People of God' --
Implications for Church Structure," also in *Christianity
Today*;[10] and "Should the Protestant Pastor be a Superstar?"
published in *The Other Side*.[11] After returning to the States
he used these articles as a base for publishing a book en-
titled, *The Problem of Wineskins*. "Leaving the North American scene and becoming involved in the work of the church in
another culture," he wrote in his preface, "prompted me to a

fundamental rethinking of the mission and structure of the church in today's world."[12]   This book was perhaps one of the most perceptive to date.

The books I have just mentioned and others such as *The Taste of New Wine*, written by Keith Miller (with an emphasis on personal renewal)[13] and *The Emerging Church*, written by Bruce Larson and Ralph Osborne (with an emphasis on corporate renewal),[14] also added emphasis to the church renewal movement.

Here and there Christian leaders experimented with new forms and structures. David Mains, "especially impressed with the writings of Elton Trueblood," launched a bold experiment in downtown Chicago. We were all impressed and excited about Circle Church, made popular by Dave's own story in his book entitled, *Full Circle*.[15]   Those of us who followed Mains' efforts, admired his willingness to confront the inner city and the problems of integration and class distinction that plagued not only our American society but the evangelical subculture.

But ultimately the experiment did not measure up to Mains' expectations and hopes. One reason which he gives himself is that he did not heed the principle being propounded by church-growth specialists regarding the need to consider structuring to reach the "homogeneous unit." Serving as a literary moderator in a dialogue between Ray Stedman and C. Peter Wagner, he stated in a recent issue of *Christianity Today* that he would "have been wise several years ago to have heeded Wagner. He warned me," Dave writes, "not to try to reach too many different people in one church. Sure enough the congregation eventually split in our attempt to extend our imperfect love too far, too fast. We were young and obsessed with solving in a few years problems that had been centuries in the making."[16]

Some (including myself) tried the house-church concept and were often disappointed and discouraged because we were ignoring twentieth-century cultural problems, such as its basic relevancy to middle-class America. Added to this were the lifestyle demands placed upon American families that soon made it a burden to continually have a home available for a church meeting, especially involving all ages. Furthermore, in these experiments we did not calculate the tremendous impact of the "church building" mentality that has evolved in our present culture, which is undeniably related to our sense of security and the need for permanence.

Some Christian leaders attempted to do away with the traditional educational ministries to children and youth so they could focus on the family. Because the first-century church did not have Sunday Schools and youth meetings, they concluded that the twentieth-century church shouldn't either, especially if it is to be a New Testament church. Again, these people ignored culture (and some continue to do so), not understanding the freedom the Holy Spirit has given us in Scripture for developing relevant forms in any culture and at any given time in history to reach biblical objectives. Furthermore, they were attempting to borrow what they felt were absolute forms from Scripture. Many were soon to learn that this approach only worked for singles and young couples without children. As soon as children came along, people graciously excused themselves and began attending a traditional church with nursery facilities and an educational program for their children. Though they often missed the dynamics generated by this kind of simple church structure, the needs of their children outweighed their own in the eventual choice of a place to worship.

With this constant exodus and/or the inability to attract families, the church was often made up of singles or young couples. This posed another problem. The church lacked mature leadership, older men who had well-ordered households who could serve as elders. Furthermore, the church lacked a dynamic that a total family brings to a body of believers.

Dr. George Peters, a missionary statesman in his own right, and who has influenced my own thinking as much as any other evangelical leader, concludes from both his biblical and worldwide cultural research that, in order to be healthy, "Churches should be built out of family units rather than individual believers."[17]

Some church renewal enthusiasts over-reacted to structure per se and attempted to design "structureless" and "leaderless" churches, which can best be illustrated in Bob Girard's work, *Brethren, Hang Loose.*[18] Though Girard did not actually think it was possible to function without form or to have groups without leaders, he seemed to convey an uneasiness when the church began to become organized. On the other hand, his concern for "body function" under the leadership of the Holy Spirit and avoiding the strong "one man" ministry is certainly noble and is, in my opinion, a very biblical emphasis. But, it represented at that time an over-reaction and swing of the pendulum away from the institutional syndrome.

During this time some traditional churches, avoiding over-
reactions, began to make significant changes. Peninsula Bible
Church in Palo Alto, California, is a prime example. Under
the leadership of Ray Stedman, this church popularized the
"body life service." Stedman's book, *Body Life*, spread the
concept and encouraged numerous traditional churches to in-
corporate more body function into their structures.[19] Ray's
ministry certainly inspired me personally. In fact, prior
to helping to start Fellowship Bible Church in Dallas, I flew
to Palo Alto and personally videotaped PBC's "body life
service" for personal viewing and study in the courses I was
teaching at Dallas Theological Seminary. (See footnote 20
for books written during this time that tell the story of
various churches that were making significant changes in
their structures.)

A Simultaneous Influence -- "Big is Better"

Almost ironically, another strong movement began basically
at the same time with the quest for church renewal we've just
described. While many were questioning the traditional approaches to church structure, both educationally and for the
total congregation, Elmer Towns began to promote the traditional Sunday School, capitalizing on a certain segment of
evangelical Christianity. When Richards and many others were
questioning the validity of the traditional Sunday School as
a significant contribution to church nurture, Towns published
a book entitled, *The Bright Future of the Sunday School*.[21]
The same year he published *The Ten Largest Sunday Schools
and What Makes Them Grow*.[22]

Towns' emphasis was destined to be more than a Sunday
School influence. It involved pastors, since one of his
findings was that "great pastors" create "great Sunday Schools"
and "great Sunday Schools" create "great churches."

The importance of the pastor as *the* leader of the church
is perhaps best illustrated when analyzing America's largest
Sunday School at that time. Wrote Towns:

> Dr. Billington is the leader of the church. He feels
> that God has called him to this position and his respon-
> sibility is a great one. He is chairman of the church
> board by virtue of the fact that he founded the church.
> When asked the question, "Do you have a Finance Com-
> mittee?" Dr. Billington replied, "You're looking at
> him."[23]

Towns was able to capture the imagination of numerous church leaders, primarily because he had a channel and public expression for his research statistics and conclusions in *Christian Life* magazine. Corresponding with his own publications, he began to promote large Sunday Schools, their statistical growth, and how they ranked in both size and growth rate. And perhaps, most significantly, he identified each pastor.

From a worldly point of view, this was an ingenious idea, building on an inherent motivational technique. Unfortunately, the primary emphasis was on numerical growth. It fostered unhealthy competition and catered significantly to the human ego and in some instances generated unethical reporting of statistics.

Another unfortunate thing occurred. As reported by William J. Peterson in *Eternity* the first of this year, many

Smaller churches which followed the example of super-aggressive evangelism and spent money for buses, television, church campuses, larger facilities (even salaries of church evangelists), often did not fare so well. Three churches in Jacksonville, Florida, recently went bankrupt. A conservative estimate indicates more than five hundred in the United States followed this example.[24]

The Church Growth Movement

Another simultaneous movement began with the church renewal movement and Towns' "bigger is better" promotional campaign. It is known as the "official" church growth movement, involving such notables as Donald A. McGavran, Win Arn, and[25] Peter Wagner. Writing[26] such books as *How to Grow a Church*,[27] *Your Church Can Grow,* and *Ten Steps for Church Growth,* these men took a more sophisticated approach to this process. Applying good techniques of research, they surfaced numerous principles which cause church growth.

Though their findings and reporting emphasized a need for solid biblical evangelism and nurture, the emphasis and practical outworking of this emphasis is still focused on quantitative growth. Though they attempt to integrate biblical principles with scientific guidelines, emphasizing the need for qualitative Christian experience, the pragmatic and the scientific often overshadow the scriptural. It appears they purposely focus on *general* ecclesiological principles

so as to relate to a wide variety of churches on the evangelical continuum.

The fact is, however, these men and many inspired by them,
plus the magazine, *Church Growth -- America*, has had a significant influence on churches and Christian leaders. Keen insights from culture and sophisticated research methodology
make this movement commendable, particularly in terms of
helping reach more people for Christ.

THE PRESENT AND THE FUTURE

No one can doubt that at this present hour evangelical
Christianity as a movement in America is well-known and popular. George Gallup, Jr.'s latest religious research projected 1978 as another "Year of the Evangelical." It has
indeed been that. Furthermore, he predicted "a continued
upsurge of evangelical strength."[28] Richard Quebedeaux in
The Worldly Evangelicals adds to this analysis when he says:

The evangelicals are a talking point everywhere. Their
growing churches, highly visible campus ministries,
phenomenally successful publishing and other media efforts, and unlikely "twice born" national celebrities
... have caught the eye of Protestant liberals, Roman
Catholics, and secular journalists.[29]

Where, however, is the church headed in its functions and
forms? What can we expect in days to come, should Jesus
Christ tarry?

From this point forward in this paper, I must bear more
personal responsibility for what I say in that these projections represent more of my own thinking than the historical
sketch I have just presented.

At the beginning of the decade Bob E. Patterson edited a
rather extensive work entitled, *The Stirring Giant*, which,
as his subtitle suggests, were the "renewal forces at work
in the modern church."[30] This book included excerpts on
church renewal from almost every published document written
on the subject.[31]

Over the last eight years it has been possible to observe
and study that "stirring giant." Though it began in groups
that would, in some respects, be on the periphery of evangelical Christianity, it very quickly spread into the center
of the circle. For several years it led to a flurry of

activity -- articles, books, and experiments. But almost
simultaneously it was overshadowed by the church-growth movement. At the same time the radical anti-institutional movements in the culture at large began to subside, which even
made some radical evangelicals more content with the institutional church. Further impetus was added by the "Jesus
Movement" -- in a sense a quasi-return by the youth culture
to institutional structures for security and hope. The charismatic renewal movement also added greatly to this impetus,
particularly in the more mainline denominations that were
characteristically void of both good Bible teaching and relational Christianity. It became clear to everyone that evangelicals were becoming a force in society to be reckoned with.
For many of us, this was no time to splinter and divide, but
to forget our differences and unite for the glory of God.
Many writers who had been critical of the church now began
to see in the rebirth of evangelicalism potential answers to
their concerns.

Unfortunately, not every Christian leader sees evangelical
popularity as a reason to rejoice. All of us are certainly
happy to be a part of a growing and recognized movement.
It's ego satisfying and provides an element of security in a
world where we have often been classified as an "Evangelical
who?" But many are concerned with what is really happening
below the surface of all of this activity.

David Wells, professor of Church History at Trinity Evangelical Divinity school, may be overstating the case somewhat
in his article in *Christianity Today* entitled, "The Gospel of
Razzmatazz," but his point is one we must ponder carefully:

> Evangelicals have never been so numerous; the im-
> pact of Christian values on society has seldom been
> less. Within evangelicalism itself scarcely ever has
> there been so much activity, but seldom ever has it
> amounted to less. Is this, one wonders, a tale sig-
> nifying nothing, though full of sound and fury?

> The current impotence of evangelicalism in the
> face of our secular culture can be analyzed from many
> angles, but one aspect that should not be overlooked
> is the level of spirituality within evangelicalism.
> Is it possible, after all, that God might have gotten
> a bit lost in all the razzmatazz? That is a sobering
> thought.[32]

Personally, I tend to agree with Wells. When our corporate and personal lifestyle is measured by biblical criteria, we come up "wanting." But I also believe that the "giant is still stirring," and it will continue to stir until it rises to stand tall in the midst of our various evangelical activities. In fact, I believe the present popularity of evangelicalism will contribute to that divine "stirring." Church renewal's initial gasp for new life at the beginning of this decade has been rather intermittent, experimental, and inadequate. It has reflected more theory that practice. It has lacked a proper biblical, historical, and cultural base. Furthermore, these efforts have been overshadowed by a burst of energy in many of our old forms. Nevertheless, what we see all about us in evangelicalism will -- I predict -- begin to subside, or at least move in different directions, primarily because of the superficial results that are being produced.

Though Findley Edge has become more optimistic about the church since he wrote his first book on renewal (which is reflected in a later book entitled, *The Greening of the Church*),[33] I have yet to read a better analysis of creeping institutionalism than in *A Quest for Vitality in Religion*. Frankly, I feel the introductory chapters in this book are more relevant today than they were fifteen years ago; primarily because of evangelical popularity.

The process of institutionalism is well-known and analyzed in the secular world. John W. Gardner, past president of the Carnegie Corporation, has said, "Like people and plants, organizations have a life cycle. They have a green and supple youth, a time of flourishing strength, and a gnarled old age."[34]

This observation is relevant to the church and any other organization that calls itself Christian. Because it has to do with structure and form, the dynamics in the process pervade any movement, secular or religious. There are definite stages in the process. A movement usually begins with vigor and dynamic inception and moves along -- unless interrupted by certain drastic crises -- until it reflects lifeless formality

Edge traces the basic steps in institutional decay, particularly as it relates to religious life:

1. Generally a movement is born in a time of great stress as a violent reaction against errors, abuses, and the injustices in the status quo.

2. If the movement is to survive this determined opposition, it must eventually organize its own
institutions.

3. In the next stage the movement passes from rejection to toleration and finally to acceptance by society.

4. Then the movement does not merely experience acceptance, it becomes popular.

5. For the sake of efficiency in organization and administration, during this period of popular growth,
there is a definite trend towards centralization of
authority.

6. Finally, we come to the last stage of the movement.
Beliefs become crystallized into dogma demanding acceptance.

7. Then, a new movement must break through those
shackles with new ideas, new beliefs, new values,
and a new way.[35]

Though what Edge has written certainly flashes yellow caution lights at evangelical popularity, it speaks even more
clearly to those of us who are leaders in separate organizations, whether they be church or parachurch in nature. Perhaps most evangelical organizations are at step #4 (acceptance and popularity); others have reached step #5 (centralization of authority); and others are already at step #6
(methodological dogmatism and indoctrination). Church renewal in evangelicalism at large actually began as step #7
nearly a decade ago and has been quietly and steadily on the
move. Though it has been overshadowed by a flurry of activity and numerical growth, the "giant is still stirring."

How do we recognize institutionalism in evangelical Christianity? Again, Edge hits the target when he outlines the
following symptoms:

1. Religion becomes institutionalized when its adher-
ents are related primarily to the church as an institution or to the organizations of the church rather
than to the living God.

2. Religion becomes institutionalized when the church
turns its concern inward upon itself, when it is more

concerned with its own existence and progress than it
is with the mission for which it was founded.

3. Religion becomes institutionalized when means become ends and ends become means. Institutions and organizations which were designed and intended to be used
as a means of serving people may become ends, and the
loyalty of people is determined by their service to
the institution.

4. Religion becomes institutionalized when it is more
concerned with the correctness of one's belief than it
is with the quality of one's life.

5. Religion becomes institutionalized when the "spirit"
of religion is lost and only the form remains.[36]

All of the phrases and symptoms as listed are recognizable
in Christian organizations today, particularly in those that
are more legalistically oriented. But it is a pervasive
problem, even among those who would be offended if classified
as "fundamentalistic." It's time we took a fresh look at our
philosophy of ministry in the light of a fresh study of *Scripture, history,* and *culture.* It is the only way to thwart the
dangers of "dry rot" in our Christian organizations. And it
can be thwarted. Structural renewal *is* possible. Again, let
me quote John W. Gardner:

Organizations differ from people and plants in that
their cycle isn't even approximately predictable. An
organization may go from youth to old age in two or
three decades, or it may last for centuries. More
important, it may go through a period of stagnation
and then revive. In short, decline is not inevitable.
Organizations need not stagnate. They often do, to
be sure, but that is because the arts of organizational renewal are not yet widely understood. Organizations can renew themselves continuously.[37]

If this be true in secular organizations, how much more so
in the church and other Christian institutions? We not only
can draw from the principles of social science but from the
authoritative Scriptures themselves.

BIBLICAL CONCERNS ABOUT THE AVERAGE CHURCH

It is impossible to draw significant lessons from history
and culture because of space and time. But let me share some

concerns regarding what I believe represent a violation of
biblical principles by many evangelical leaders. I further
believe that a correct application of these principles is
absolutely essential to break through the shackles wherever
Christianity has become institutionalized. Though the church
will be our primary focus in the statement of these concerns,
they apply equally to all Christian organizations.

1. Our Criteria for Evaluating Success

   Evangelical Christians today, as a whole, appear "numbers"
oriented. The Bible certainly illustrates numerical growth,
but clearly focuses on qualitative growth as a measure of
success, both personally and corporately. The criteria for
personal growth is summarized in Paul's qualification profile for spiritual leaders in I Timothy 3 and Titus 1. The
criteria was the degree of *faith*, *hope*, and *love* reflected by
each local body of believers (see Eph. 1:15-18; Col. 1:3-5;[38]
I Thess. 1:2-3; II Thess. 1:3-4).

2. Our Church Structures Must Provide Believers with
   Balanced Christian Experience in Order to Produce
   Balanced Christians

   John Stott said it well when he wrote about the church's
priorities.

> First, we need a preaching and teaching ministry
> that faithfully expounds the text of Scripture at the
> same time it relates to the burning issues of the day
> ... Second, we need a warm, caring, supportive fellow-
> ship ... Thirdly, we need worship services that express
> the reality of the living God and joyfully celebrate
> Jesus Christ's victory over sin and death ... Fourthly,
> we need an outreach to the secular community that is[39]
> imaginative, sensitive, and compassionate.

   These priorities grow directly out of the New Testament
and are best illustrated in Acts 2:42-47. I prefer to call
them three vital experiences which Christians need, inter-
relating relationships with one another (*koinonia*) and relationships with God (worship). Stated this way, they are as
follows:

   1. A vital learning experience with the Word of God.
   2. Vital relational experiences --
       -- with God
       -- with one another

3. A vital witnessing experience with the unsaved world, which should be both corporate and personal.

A careful study of churches today reflects the fact that church leaders have used their biblical freedom in church form, but unfortunately we tend to structure for one or two of these experiences and usually not all three. Results in believers' lives are very obvious:

First, churches that structure for *Bible teaching* (I affectionately call these the little "Bible institutes"), but exclude *fellowship* and *evangelism*, soon become cold and academic.

Second, churches that structure for *fellowship* (the relational churches), but neglect solid *Bible teaching* and *sharing Christ,* soon become superficial and emotional.

Third, churches that structure for *evangelism* (the great soul-winning churches), but neglect *Bible teaching* and *fellowship,* are filled with people starved for the Word of God and hungry for deep relationships.

Fourth, churches that structure for *Bible teaching* and *fellowship*, but neglect *evangelism,* become ingrown and stagnant.

Fifth, churches that structure for *Bible teaching* and *evangelism*, but neglect *relational* Christianity, produce Christians who do know the Word but never feel comfortable in developing deep relationships with others. Consequently, they also feel uncomfortable with non-Christians. They are the "soul saving" people, but they have difficulty relating to these individuals as *total* human beings.

Sixth, churches that structure for *fellowship* and *evangelism* and neglect *Bible teaching* are the most hazardous, for they often cause Christians to get off into false doctrine and into cultic groups.

The challenge that faces the church of tomorrow -- both old and new -- is to develop contemporary structures that make it culturally convenient for Christians to have *all three* of these experiences and in proper balance. It is only then that we will produce qualitative results in the lives of believers.

3. We Must Practice the Principle of Multiple Leadership
   in the Church

The "one man" ministry is, I feel, the most dangerous
trend in evangelical churches today. Not only is it a reflection of creeping institutionalism, but it is dangerous
for several reasons:

First, it is a violation of a biblical principle, and when
we violate Scripture, it always leads to ultimate problems.

Second, though the "one man" ministry may and has produced
qualitative biblical results, it will ultimately lead to serious problems. For one thing, a work that is built around a
very talented individual will not endure ultimately, particularly if the work grows large and the man is an unusually
gifted person.

Third, some men who tend to be individualistic and authoritarian in their leadership style, even as evangelical Christians, often reflect serious personality problems, which, in
turn, are reflected through their people. There are many
vivid illustrations of this today.

Though it is certainly an unfair comparison to equate any
evangelical leader with Jim Jones, there is something frightening about Dr. Stefan Pasternack's analysis of those who be-
longed to the People's Temple in Guyana. Speaking of these
people, and quoted in *Time* magazine, he said:

> They have a desire to be part of something meaning-
> ful. In joining, they regress and relax their per-
> sonal judgments to the point that they are supplanted
> by the group's often primitive feelings. With a sick
> leader, these primitive feelings are intensified and
> get worse. The members develop a total identity with
> the leader and in the process take on his sickness.[40]

As I read this article, I could not help but recognize some
of these same symptoms in some Bible-believing churches. It
is my personal opinion that God designed multiple leadership
as a safeguard against this kind of tendency. God does in-
tend to use leaders, but His plan is also clearly specified
that we are to develop others who serve with us with equal
authority, although they may not have the same degree of
responsibility.

A *fourth* danger in the "one man" approach is that older
and more experienced men who have built great churches around
their own strengths and abilities are teaching younger men
they can do it, too. In many instances this leads to unbelievable failure and heartache, for both the would-be pastor
and the people he has tried to lead.

4. We Must Focus on Scriptural Principles, not Cultural
   Patterns

The great danger today is to attempt to transport successful forms and structures from one subculture to another, without understanding the principles that undergird these patterns
and how to creatively apply them in different situations.
More than any one thing, this leads to institutionalized
Christianity.

A FINAL PROJECTION

I believe evangelical churches will experience more renewal in the days to come than ever before. However, it will
be beyond the experimental stage. It will be based on more
adequate biblical and historical and cultural insights. It
will not represent change for change's sake. More and more
churches will come into existence with totally new forms that
are built on biblical principles. Many old, established
churches will follow suit in making form changes, but at a
much slower rate. However, as time passes, the change rate
will speed up because more and more churches will be modeling the process of renewal. Furthermore, the continuing
changes in the culture at large will also help people to
feel more secure with change.

The "big one man churches" syndrome will wane, although
it will always be a problem in our society, primarily because
of the secular models in our culture. People will always borrow techniques and strategies from the world without carefully
evaluating them in the light of the scriptural principles.

However, the super-churches that are extremely "man
centered" will eventually run out of steam. Many people
will grow tired of high-pressure tactics and treadmill-type
activities. Many will become religious dropouts, disillusioned with Christianity. Others will find new churches
with more balanced and authentic Christianity.

In conclusion, I believe the future is very bright for
the church. Our greatest asset today is that people still

believe the Bible -- even many church dropouts, which is[41]
clear from the 1978 Gallup poll of unchurched Americans.
And when people believe the Bible, we can use that platform
to lead them into a biblical understanding of what God intended the church to be. The opportunity is there. What we
do with it will depend upon our faithfulness in carrying out
God's will for our lives.

One last projection, which is not directly related to the
purpose of this paper, but is closely aligned with the future
forms of the church. We will see in the future a gradual
move in the direction of institutional renewal and changes
in our Bible college and seminary structures. We will see
more clearly than ever the need to develop approaches to curriculum building and teaching that are uniquely designed to
apply biblical principles, rather than borrowing structures
from the world's educational systems that are primarily designed for cognative input. But that is another "chapter"
for future discussion. But as these changes take place,
it will also speed up the process of renewal in the local
church.

FOOTNOTES

[1]Kenneth Kantzer, "Interview," *Christianity Today* (April 7, 1978), p. 24.

[2]Gene A. Getz, *Sharpening the Focus of the Church* (Chicago: Moody Press, 1974).

[3]Elton Trueblood, *The Company of the Committed* (Harper Brothers, 1961), p. 5. (Quoted from Karl Heim *Christian Faith and Natural Science* [New York: Harper Brothers, 1957] p. 24).

[4]Findley B. Edge, *A Quest for Vitality in Religion* (Nashville: Broadman Press, 1963), p. 9.

[5]Larry Richards, *A New Face for the Church* (Grand Rapids: Zondervan Publishing House, 1970), p. 9

[6]Francis Schaeffer, *The Church at the End of the Twentieth Century* (Downers Grove: Inter Varsity Press, 1970), p. 67.

[7]Howard Snyder, "The Fellowship of the Holy Spirit," *Christianity Today* (November 6, 1970), pp. 4-7.

[8]_____, "Church Renewal Through Small Groups," *United Evangelical Action* (Summer, 1971), pp. 29-31.

[9]_____, "Does the Church Suffer an Edifice Complex?" *World Vision* (September, 1971), pp. 4-5.

[10]_____, "'The People of God' -- Implications for Church Structure," *Christianity Today* (October 27, 1972), pp. 6-11.

[11]_____, "Should the Protestant Pastor be a Superstar?" *The Other Side* (March-April, 1973), pp. 8-11.

[12]_____, *The Problem of Wineskins* (Downers Grove: Inter Varsity Press, 1975), p. 11.

[13]Keith Miller, *The Taste of New Wine* (Waco: Word Books Publisher, 1975).

[14]Bruce Larson and Ralph Osborne, *The Emerging Church* (Waco: Word Books Publisher, 1970).

[15]David Mains, *Full Circle* (Waco: Word Books Publishers, 1971), p. 22.

[16]_____, "A Balanced Stride," *Christianity Today* (August 18, 1978), p. 15.

[17]George W. Peters, *Saturation Evangelism* (Grand Rapids: Zondervan Publishing House, 1972).

[18]Robert Girard, *Brethren Hang Loose* (Grand Rapids: Zondervan Publishing House, 1972).

[19]Ray Stedman, *Body Life* (Glendale: Regal Books, 1972).

[20]Dan Baumann, *All Originality Makes a Dull Church* (Santa Ana: Vision House Publisher, 1976).

Bernard Palmer, *Pattern for a Total Church* (Wheaton: Victor Books, 1973).

Larry Richards, *Three Churches in Renewal* (Grand Rapids: Zondervan Publishing House, 1975).

Mike Tucker, *The Church That Dared to Change* (Wheaton: Tyndale House, 1975).

[21]Elmer Towns, *The Bright Future of the Sunday School* (Minneapolis: F.C. Publications, 1969).

[22]_____, *The Ten Largest Sunday Schools and What Makes Them Grow* (Grand Rapids: Baker Book House, 1965).

[23]*Ibid*, p. 20.

[24]William J. Petersen, "Thinking Big," *Eternity* (February, 1978), p. 21.

[25]Donald A. McGavran, *How To Grow a Church* (Glendale: Regal Books, 1973).

[26]C. Peter Wagner, *Your Church Can Grow* (Glendale: Regal Books, 1976).

[27]Donald A. McGavran and Winfield C. Arn, *Ten Steps for Church Growth* (New York: Harper and Row Publishers, 1977).

[28]Albert J. Menendez, "Who Are the Evangelicals?" *Christianity Today* (January 27, 1978), p. 42.

[29] Richard Quebedeaux, *The Worldly Evangelicals* (New York: Harper and Row Publishers, 1978), p. 3.

[30] Bob E. Patterson (Editor), *The Stirring Giant* (Waco: Word Books, 1971).

[31] In a book entitled *Contemporary Christian Trends*, edited by William M. Pinson, Jr., and Clyde E. Fant, Jr., Elton Trueblood contributed a chapter entitled, "The Renewal Movement." Regarding when the current renewal movement began, he states that it paralleled the decline in interest in ecumenical efforts (pp. 12, 13).

[32] David Wells, "The Gospel of Razzmatazz," *Christianity Today* (April 7, 1978), pp. 32-33.

[33] Findley B. Edge, *The Greening of a Church* (Waco: Word Books Publisher, 1971).

[34] John W. Gardner, "How to Prevent Organizational Dry Rot," *Harper's* (October, 1965), p. 20

[35] Findley B. Edge, *A Quest for Vitality in Religion* (Nashville: Broadman Press, 1963).

[36] *Ibid*, pp. 23-26.

[37] John W. Gardner, op. cit.

[38] I have personally written about these criteria in four books: *The Measure of a Man* (1974); *The Measure of a Church* (1975); *The Measure of a Family* (1976); and *The Measure of a Woman* (1977). All of these books have been published by Regal. I developed these materials from my ministry with people at Fellowship Bible Church and its branches in Dallas.

[39] John R. Stott, "Unhooked Christians," *Christianity Today* (October 7, 1977), pp. 40-41.

[40] "Why People Join," *Time* (December 4, 1978), p. 27.

[41] "The Unchurched: Believers at Heart?" *Christianity Today* (July 21, 1978), p. 52.

RECENT ARTICLES RELATED TO THE
FUTURE OF THE CHURCH,
BUT NOT QUOTED IN THIS PAPER

[1]Paul Benjamin, "The Urgency of the Equipping Ministry," *Christianity Today* (September 22, 1978), pp. 21-22.

[2]Michael Harper, "Duplicating the New Testament Church," *Eternity* (April, 1978), pp. 24-25, 37.

[3]George A. Huber, "The Evangelical's Day of Popularity," *Christianity Today* (February 10, 1978), p. 32.

[4]Carl H. Lundquist, "Journey to Renewal," *Christianity Today* (January 13, 1978), pp. 13-17.

[5]Donald McGavran, "Support of the Church for the Good of Society," *Christianity Today* (April 7, 1978), pp. 38-39.

[6]_____, (An interview with McGavran by Charles Arn,) *Church Growth: America* (Summer, 1977), pp. 8-9, 22.

[7]David Mains, "Can My Church Be Changed?" *Eternity* (August, 1978), pp. 12-16.

[8]Leon Morris, "A Good Word for the Institution," *Christianity Today* (March 10, 1978), pp. 81-83.

[9]Charles Mylander, "A Glimpse in the Crystal Ball," *Church Growth: America* (Summer, 1978), pp. 14-15.

[10]Donald Tinder, "Why the Evangelical Upswing?" *Christianity Today* (October 21, 1977), pp. 10-12.

[11]Tom Wolf, "Oikos Evangelism -- The Biblical Pattern" *Church Growth: America* (January-February, 1978), pp. 11-13.

[12]_____, "The Church in a Changing Community" *Church Growth: America* (January-February, 1977), pp. 23-26.

The Future of the Church: Its Nurture, Form, and Function

Response: Gordon MacDonald

Dr. Getz is the first, I think, of four speakers who will be chatting in the next day on some aspect or another of what is called, in general, "The Future of the Church." I suspect that the people who planned this conference gave him an almost impossible task as being the first of these four speakers. And what I sense he attempted to do -- rather than spend all of his time looking to the future -- was to "bring us up to speed" so we can more intelligently wrestle with the data that is going to be laid before us in the coming day.

As I listened to this paper, I was impressed, first of all, by all that he observed in the last fifteen or eighteen years, which is the general span of time in which I have been a pastor. I vividly remember in the early sixties, when I first went to seminary, that the general attitude of most seminary students was, "I will be anything but a pastor -- I will go anywhere but to the church." It was a "low moment." And it is exciting now to follow Dr. Getz's comments tonight and see that over these last fifteen years there has been an enormous resurgence -- some negative, some positive -- in the awareness of the place of the church in the Kingdom and where it is going in the future

In prefacing all of his remarks to bring us up to speed for the next day, Gene Getz, first of all, took on some assumptions with which I think we are probably all in agreement. I can't imagine that we would have any problems with

them, but let me just very quickly remind you of some of the
things he said:

-- The congregation is never static, he reminded us, in
   terms of form -- I guess form would be the best way
   -- and function is always in the process of change.

-- Secondly, he reminded us that the Bible gives to us
   as church men and women enduring *principles* rather
   than *prescriptions* as to how a church should act or
   how it should form itself.

-- Then he made an extreme emphasis upon the fact that
   the Scriptures give us a record of the functions of
   a congregation and perhaps, in his opinion, tend to
   negate or leave out many of the earlier functions
   so that we are not bound to one particular cultural
   setting.

I thought it was insightful also in this list of assumptions that he reminded us that often the church, in its message and ministry, responds to "spill overs" from the culture
around us. I would wish that the church of which I am a part
had been far more *instigative* in, for example, calling our
government to a purity in the Watergate era or that the church
would have had more to say about the role of women in the culture before the secularists started the ball rolling. I would
have wished the church would have *led* on the matter of race
and on the matter of the starvation problem in the world. And
I am praying that somehow we as "church persons" -- if that is
the new word -- will find a way to lead the world on the whole
question of simplicity in lifestyle. But, unfortunately, we
tend in this century to be more reactionary than initiative in
these matters. And so, I accept his assumption that often
changes in the church are the result of spill-overs from
the culture.

Probably the most valuable part of Dr. Getz's paper was
the attempt, first of all, to take us on a trek from the
past up to the present, namely, in the sixties and seventies.
He recalled for us three basic things:

1. The anti-institutional mood which launched this whole
era and gave birth in our own backyard to the church-renewal
movement a la Trueblood and others, calling for reappraisal
of forms and structures.

2. At the same time he reminded us about the growth of the "bigger is better" movement, which I can understand.

3. And also, he gave us an interesting appraisal for a moment or two on the church-growth movement and suggested to us something I emphatically agree on: the church-growth movement too often pragmatically falls into a study of *quantitative* growth rather than *qualitative* growth in the church.

From the present to the future, he reminded us of the stirring giant: this evangelical resurgence. And I think I heard him say at this point, that it's all very exciting, but it's too early to tell exactly where it's going. It's probable that, as the days go by, many of the big things which are happening today are going to die out and perhaps will leave in their wake some of the more purified qualities in which the congregation concept can grow in the seventies or the eighties and nineties.

He closed his paper by warning us of several things -- and again I find it easy to identify with these things; I wish I had been able to say them the same way he did:

-- He warns us of a crippling criteria for success in which the "American way" of defining success often infiltrates our value system wherein numbers speak louder than anything else. And he looks optimistically to the possibility that there are Christians now here and there who are looking more for the *quality* growth of the human spirit as it's touched by the power of the Holy Spirit rather than *how many numbers* are generated.

-- I could not agree with him more in his second comment that we desperately need to look into the future and project congregations which are preaching a "balanced Gospel." In his paper he mentioned a balanced Gospel at least from three perspectives: the aspect of *learning* congregations, *relating* congregations, and *witnessing* congregations. If I were to challenge or to act in rebuttal -- and that is not necessarily the job of responders this year -- I would have wished that he would have said a little bit more about the *worshipping* congregations. For I feel that if there is anywhere in evangelicalism we are dramatically deficient these days, it is *how* to worship the living and true God.

-- I think I heard him warning us implicitly through
those words that evangelicalism has been too often
marked with just the act of evangelism rather than
the longer and more "dig deeper" job of bringing
Christians to maturity. Matured *implies* evangelism, but it certainly goes far beyond simply leading people to Christ. This is richly expressed
in Colossians 1:28 and 29.

-- Finally, he closes with warnings about the future
in the conception of *multiple leadership* as op-
posed to the so-called *"one man church"* -- which
really should be the "one person" church, given
our nomenclature these days, I suppose (that is
thrown in for free -- supposedly humorous). I am
not as concerned about *one-man* leadership as I am
concerned about *accountable* leadership. I am not
too sure that we will ever see dramatic leadership
from a *committee* or a *plurality of people who share
authority equally*. If multiple leadership is the
leadership of different people with different gifts,
then I fall into line quickly. I also share the
tremendous concern of the almost unbridled, unac-
countable one-man leadership in both churches and
parachurch organizations -- a very serious matter.

Coming to conclusion, I am going to suggest to you tonight
that Dr. Getz has brought us up to a starting line of moving
into the future in our discussion and perhaps has set in motion the atmosphere for asking several questions:

1. First of all, this matter of the *nurture* or *the nature
of the church*. Some are suggesting that the evangelical
church is facing an enormous crisis in the eighties in deter-
mining what it is itself -- or the whole question of ecclesiology. I am impressed with Robert Webber's book, *Common
Roots*, in his suggestion -- or his hint -- that perhaps we
are living in the last days of the Reformation, and the
Reformation itself revolved more or less on one doctrinal
presentation, the doctrine of justification by grace. And
it may be that in the coming years one of the hard questions
the church will have to ask itself all over again is, "What
is our essential nature as the church?" Are we a prophetic
body speaking to the world about God's design of life by the
way we live and the things we say -- or are we simply an en-
clave that retreats from the wickedness of the world and
awaits the Lord's coming? What is our ecclesiological substance and nature in the future? And that, I predict, is

going to be one of the great questions of the age, springing
from some of the comments I have heard tonight.

   2. Secondly, a *question about form*: What is the church
going to be like in the eighties and nineties? Is there
strength, as some suggest, in the unrestrained breeding of
organizations and dreams where everyone can conceivably be
a founder and director and, I suspect, therefore, take the
risk of engendering Jim Joneses type?

   3. Or, thirdly, *in terms of functions*: How will the
church be able to flesh out its own self-perception? Is
there something coming in the eighties of a kind of coalition
between certain Roman Catholic and Protestant groups glued
together, for example, by the charismatic movement or commitments in both groups to evangelism and to relational dynamics?
Or, on the other hand, are we headed in the eighties and
nineties toward a proliferation of orders from which there
may emerge some undefinable future consensus in the church?

   Finally, having taken all this, several other smaller questions which ought to be wrestled with by our groups:

   -- How will the church, in terms of nurture, form, and
      function, respond in the eighties and nineties to
      the conceivable possibilities that we will face legal
      parameters as the government is forced to take more
      and more careful perception of cults and so forth
      and various independent religious organizations?

   -- How will the church react if we lose our tax-shelter
      privileges?

   -- How will the church react if our culture goes to a
      four-day work-week?

   -- How will we be affected by the growing rise of cor-
      porate and community agencies which are really, from
      a secular perspective, doing more and more of what
      I could call pastoral-care ministries?

   -- And, finally, how will we face the acceleration of
      costs as they pertain to salaries, to buildings,
      property, parking lots, etc.?

   And, in conclusion, I will simply say -- and I think Dr.
Getz was saying this in his own conclusion, and I agree with
him -- a lot of it comes down to our problems of how are we

going to train our young men and women for ministry in the eighties and nineties in our seminaries? It is going to come down to the *courage of the present generation of evangelical leadership* and, *finally, how we ourselves submit ourselves to the accountability of the body of Christ.*

The Future of the Church: The Christian Family

Address: Armand M. Nicholi, Jr.

The word "family" has many definitions. For our purposes this morning we will use the term to mean simply "parents and their children" -- the so-called nuclear family we hear so much about today. The topic given me included the term "Christian family," and I will define that arbitrarily as a family where one or both parents embrace the Christian faith and attempt to foster and reflect that faith in their family activities. One can, of course, raise many objections to these definitions -- for example, in the United States only one household in three consists of parents and their children -- one-parent families are growing about twenty times faster than two-parent families.

If we take little time to refine our definition of the family, we will take even less time to comment on the family's profound significance to the moral, emotional, mental, and spiritual development of the individual as well as society as a whole.

As human beings we all share the experience of being a child and, for good or evil, spending the days of our childhood in the context of the family. Here the seed is sown for what we become as adults -- for the inner picture we develop of ourselves, for how we see others and feel about them, for our concept of right and wrong, for our capacity to establish the close, warm, sustained relationships we all desire as well as the intimate sexual relationships necessary to have a family of our own, for our attitude toward authority and our capacity to resolve our ambivalence toward it, especially toward the ultimate authority in our lives, for the way we attempt to make sense out of our existence on this planet, and so forth. Once we become adults, most of us marry and begin life in a second family. As we grow older, we find ourselves as grandparents and part of still another family. So, for most of us most of our lives are lived within the framework of the family. No human interaction has greater impact on our lives than our family experience.

For several years now we have been warned by social scientists that because of forces within and without, the family is disintegrating and may well not survive this century. Several books published in the seventies have criticized the family and have implied that this process of disintegration ought to be helped along. In a book titled, *The Death of the Family*, a British physician suggests doing away with the family because it is a primary conditioning device for the maintenance of a Western, imperialistic world view. In the book, *Sexual Politics*, a feminist writes that the family must go because it is the chief institution in contemporary society that oppresses and enslaves women. This idea reflects most of the women's liberation literature of the seventies that describes marriage as passe, denegrates the role of wife and mother, and welcomes the breakdown of the family because it "is the prime barrier to radical social change."

Is there real danger that the American family will cease to exist? I do not think so. Most Americans marry, have children, and commit themselves to living in a family household. And I strongly believe that they will continue to do so in the future. We do, however, have great cause for concern. Our concern is not that the family will disappear, but rather that certain trends prevalent today will incapacitate the family, destroy its integrity, and cause its members to suffer such crippling emotional conflicts that they will become not an asset but an increasing and intolerable burden to society.

Before mentioning a few of these trends, let me share with you some observations concerning the emotional health of a family and the individuals within it. If any one factor influences the character development and emotional stability of an individual, it is the quality of the relationship he experiences as a child with both of his parents. Conversely, if there is one experience that people suffering from severe emotional illness have in common, it is the absence of a parent through death, divorce, or time-demanding job. A parent's inaccessibility either physically, emotionally, or both, can exert a significant influence on the child's emotional health.

These impressions come from a vast body of clinical impressions and research data in the medical literature which began over three decades ago and that led the World Health Organization over twenty years ago to make this statement: "What is believed to be essential for mental health is that the infant and young child should experience a warm, intimate, and continuous relationship with his mother ..." and then presented evidence that indicated that many forms of psychoneuroses and character disorders are to be attributed to the absence of the mother or to discontinuities in the child's relationship with his mother. In the years following that statement, research throughout the world has demonstrated that a separation from the mother -- even for brief periods of hospitalization -- and the quality of the mother's relationship with the child, can profoundly affect both the child's physical and emotional development. And more recent research has demonstrated the full emotional impact on the child of the missing or inaccessible father.

If time permits, I would like to share some of this fascinating research with you, but suffice it now to say what has been shown over and over again to have the most profound effect on the emotional development of the child is a close, warm, sustained, and continuous relationship with *both* parents. Yet certain trends in our society make this most difficult today. Let me now mention briefly a few of these trends.

The trend toward quick and easy divorce has a strong bearing on family life in this country. The ever-increasing divorce rate subjects an ever-increasing number of children to physically and emotionally absent parents. The divorce rate has risen 700 percent in this century and continues to soar. There is now one divorce for every 1.8 marriages, and over a million children a year are involved in divorce cases.

The increasing numbers of married women who have joined the labor force and work outside of the home -- especially those mothers with young children -- have a profound effect on family life. In 1948, 18 percent of the nation's mothers worked outside of the home. In 1971 this figure jumped to 43 percent in the United States. Today it is over 50 percent, and the frequent articles describing how this phenomenon has increased marital stress and contributed to the high rate of divorce have become all too familiar. What I find to be most disturbing about this phenomenon is that an ever-increasing percentage of the mothers who work are mothers of very young children. There are nearly six million pre-school children today whose mothers work. Only a small fraction of these mothers work because of economic necessity.

The tendency of many colleges and universities in this country is to convey the notion that the role of wife and mother is passe, and to settle for such a role in life is to settle for second-class citizenship. The Women's Liberation Movement, though small in numbers, has made an impact here. Though they focus on a number of legitimate grievances, they appear geared to deny the responsibility of being a wife and mother. Though all that we know about human behavior from a vast amount of clinical research data, stresses with unmistakable clarity the importance of the presence of both parents, and especially the mother, during the first few years of life, many educated women today seem to lose sight quickly of that fact. Unless they have a career of their own they can pursue while raising a family, they consider their lives a failure. What has become unmistakably clear from my experience is that no woman can do both at the same time without sacrificing one or the other.

Another trend that imposes great stress on the American family is the tendency to move frequently. Technical advances, especially progress in transportation, has made our society extremely mobile. Human beings throughout history up to and including our grandfathers' time, traveled in their entire lifetime an average of 30,000 miles, a distance man can now travel in space in little more than an hour. The mass move from rural and small towns to urban and suburban living has produced marked changes in the quality of family life, where the children now have little contact with grandparents, aunts, and uncles in the so-called extended family. Parents who work often travel long distances as part of that work. Because of such travel, a father may be absent from home for many days or for weeks at a time. The job also frequently causes the whole family to move. Forty million Americans move each year, and according to the 1970 Census, 50 percent of the population had lived at a different address five years earlier. We have only begun to understand the enormous psychological uprooting that a move can have on the family.

The obtrusion of the television set into the American home has had an effect on the American family that we have not yet even begun to fathom. Parental inaccessibility

contributes to children spending enormous amounts of time
watching television. The television set has become a baby-
sitter in many homes. Television acts as a two-edged sword.
It both results from and causes parental inaccessibility.
When parents are home physically, television often inter-
feres with the meaningful interaction between members of the
family. When the family is together, more hours are spent
with individuals interacting with the television set than
with one another.

Television appeared in the American home a little over
two decades ago, and during the first ten years the proportion of families owning a set grew from zero to over 90 percent. We are just beginning to experience the first generation brought up completely on television. Some studies have
shown that the average viewing time of the American child
from six to sixteen years of age is between twenty and twenty-
four hours per week. If he lives to be eighty and that continues throughout his life, he will have spent eight to ten
years of his life watching television. Or to put it another
way, if he lives to be eighty, he will have lived a little
less than 30,000 days. Because he sleeps one-third of that
time, he has about 20,000 days. One-fifth of his waking life
-- or about 4,000 days -- will have been spent watching television. We have only begun to realize the full impact of
this phenomenon on family life. Research showing the effects
of violence on television on the behavior of both children
and adults has been less than encouraging.

There is still another trend affecting the family. It
concerns the lack of impulse control prevalent in our culture
today. Society seems to have given up its traditional civil-
izing task of helping to maintain control of aggressive and
sexual impulses. The deep moral confusion we have observed
over the past decade seems to have lifted all the restraints
and limits. During the past ten years, I have noticed a
marked change in the type of problems that bring young people
to a psychiatrist. Previously, a great many came because of
excessive inhibition of impulses. Today the opposite is true.
I might add here parenthetically that people in my field at-
tribute this lack of control to the declining influence of
the father in the American home. Inability to control aggression can be observed most overtly in the steady rise of violent crime in this country. In Boston, in the so-called cultural hub of the universe, where there are more people pursuing higher education than perhaps any place on earth, a
murder occurs about every third day. Aggression within the
home has been increasing steadily. Since it has been required

to report "battered child" cases, we have been observing an alarming increase in this phenomenon. Authorities expect between two to four million cases to be reported this year, and about 15,000 of these will suffer permanent brain damage; about 2,000 will die. And we believe that there are even more cases that go unreported.

The inability to control sexual impulses is even more prevalent. The number of illegitimate births in this country continues to rise with far more than one-quarter of a million each year. Twenty-one percent of all births in the United States occur in the age group between twelve and nineteen, and half of these girls are unmarried. Pregnancies in teenage girls has increased by 33 percent within the past five years. Statistics for 1974 show that over one-half million teenage pregnancies occured with one-quarter of a million terminating in abortion. That 50 percent of teenage marriages end in divorce within five years after marriage, makes these findings no less disturbing.

I have also noticed what appears to be an increased incidence of homosexuality among young people and an increased freedom in expressing homosexual impulses. I might also add here that recent research shows a statistically significant higher incidence of cold, rejecting, and inaccessible fathers within the family background of homosexuals.

These trends, I believe, create an extremely negative impact on family life -- primarily because they contribute to a change in child rearing that has been taking place in this country during the past few decades. The change is this: in American homes today child care has shifted from parents to other agencies. A home in which both parents are available to the child emotionally as well as physically has become, in some areas of our society, the exception rather than the rule. And I refer not to the disadvantaged home where the father is missing and the mother works. I refer to even the most affluent homes. Surveys of child-rearing studies in the United States by Bronfenbrenner all point to "a progressive decrease, especially in recent decades, in the amount of contact between parents and their children." Cross-cultural studies show that United States parents spend considerably less time with their children than almost any other country in the world. Although both Russian parents work and although Russian children spend a great deal of time in family collectives, emotional ties between children and parents are stronger and the time spent together considerably greater than in the United States; there is relatively little

juvenile delinquency in Russia. Some Russian fathers have
said they would never let a day go by without spending two
hours with their sons. A study in a small community in this
country of how much time fathers spend with their very young
sons shows that the average time pe⸱ day was about thirty-
seven seconds!

A child experiences an absent or an emotionally inaccessible parent as rejection, and rejection inevitably breeds
resentment and hostility. Depending on the age of the child,
particular makeup of the child, and the sex of the parent who
is missing or inaccessible, the child when he becomes an
adult may experience various kinds of crippling emotional
conflict. And all of this can occur in a Christian home as
well as a non-Christian home. Out of the hundreds of cases
that come to mind from several years of clinical practice, I
will briefly mention two because they both come from fine
Christian homes.

A young woman in her late twenties finds herself suffering from extreme anxiety and inability to form close relationships with either sex. She becomes engaged, and then for
reasons she does not understand breaks her engagement in a
state of panic. Though strikingly attractive and highly
intelligent, she feels unworthy and that others, once they
get to know her, will reject her. If others do not continually reassure her that they approve of her, she feels hostile
and then acts in a way that incurs the rejection she fears.
She consults a doctor, despondent, lonely, and confused, that
in her thirty years she has found no close satisfying relationship. With her doctor she recalls as a child being excessively dependent on a mother who was chronically depressed
and emotionally inaccessible. When the patient was seven
years old, her mother took her to a hospital and left her
there for a week to have her tonsils removed. She had no
visitors and was told later that parents were not allowed to
visit the hospital. When the girl returned home, her mother
immediately left for the hospital to deliver a younger sibling
-- who then became the focus of the limited affection the
mother had to give. So, the child grew up excessively dependent on her mother, terrified that she might be left again,
enraged for not being given to emotionally, feeling worthless,
and thus setting the stage for the suffering and frustration
she experienced as an adult.

A gifted young physician in his thirties complained of
paralyzing anxiety whenever he was with his superiors in the
hospital. He also had difficulty experiencing a sense of

peace in his relationship with God, though he professed a strong Christian faith. He was haunted by the conviction that God had ordained that at some period in his life he must suffer great physical torture. A key point in this young doctor's childhood history was that from the time he was two years old until he left for boarding school, his father would, at the slightest provocation -- such as not saying "thank you" to his mother -- take him to the bathroom, remove his trousers, and beat him with a belt until he drew blood. Then his father would pick him up and hug and kiss him, telling the boy how much he loved him. During the therapy, the patient discovered that these early experiences were not unrelated to the intense anxiety he experienced as an adult toward authority generally and toward God in particular, and that had always been so puzzling to him.

Several letters from you participants asked me to talk about the role of the father; suffice for now to say that how a child relates to his father, the first authority in his life, determines in large measure, how he competes with the world, how he handles his ambivalence toward authority generally, and, to some extent, the unconscious attitudes he carries toward the ultimate authority in his life.

These brief thumbnail sketches do not do justice to the complex dynamics that are a part of every human life -- but they illustrate briefly how an inaccessible or rejecting parent can give rise to emotional disorder later in life. If we had time to dwell further on these two illustrations, we would see two deeply committed, evangelical Christian families who produced children who grew to be adults with emotional conflicts that strongly interfered with their spiritual growth. As they resolved these conflicts, they found themselves freer to grow spiritually and to come to know God, not as their neurotic conflicts tended to distort Him, but to know Him as revealed through Scripture and through their personal experience.

From my clinical experience and from my research with college students, I began to notice (1) that a large number suffered from an incapacitating symptomatic or characterological conflict, (2) that they seemed to have in common a number of traumatic early experiences with a rejecting, inaccessible or absent parent, and (3) when we looked at their histories carefully, there appeared to be some causal relation between the earlier experiences and the emotional illness they were suffering as an adult. About ten years ago I began studying a large group of young men, about 1500 who had dropped out

of Harvard for psychiatric reasons. Two characteristics of
the group were (1) a marked isolation and alienation from
their parents, especially their fathers, and (2) an overwhelming apathy and lack of motivation. In addition, among
those who dropped out for psychiatric reasons who had the
most serious illness, that is, those hospitalized and diag-
nosed as schizophrenic, a large number had lost one or both
parents through death; when compared with several control
groups, this finding proved highly significant statistically,
and this provided me with my first clue that there might be
a relationship between a missing parent and emotional illness.
As I began to work with patients clinically, I began to realize that absence through death was only the *most severe* kind
of absence, that there were many other kinds of absence --
that a parent could be physically present and still be emotionally absent or inaccessible. Over the past few years,
research studies have been carried out throughout the world,
trying to refine our understanding of this phenomena and trying to understand why some children are paralyzed by these
experiences and others seem to be unaffected (in the same
way some people are paralyzed by polio and others are not).
The research is fascinating, and we could spend several hours
discussing it.

Because so many of the questions you sent to me concerned
the role of the father, I will mention one or two research
findings concerning the absent father. In studies with in-
fants, we now know that a father evokes very specific responses that differ markedly from contact with the mother,
and that his presence or absence has a specific influence on
the psychological development of the very young child. Studies on missing fathers have been carried out in several different countries. I will mention but one here in the United
States. In a study published in the *Archives of General
Psychiatry* in 1973, a study was made of the periodic absence
of the father on 200 patients at a military medical clinic
where the father's absence was due to his military occupation.
The children ranged from three to eighteen years of age.

The researchers found early reaction to the father's de-
parture resembled reactions to children who lose a father by
death: (1) rageful protest over desertion, (2) denial of
the loss and an intense fantasy relationship with the parent,
(3) efforts at reunion, (4) irrational guilt and a need for
punishment, (5) exaggerated separation anxieties and fears
of being abandoned, (6) a decrease in impulse control, and
(7) a wide variety of regressive symptoms.

When the father left home, the child was often allowed to do things not otherwise permitted. This made it difficult for the child to internalize a consistent set of standards for controlling his behavior. In several instances, the father's leaving was followed by disobedience, decline in school performance, and aggressive antisocial behavior. The child seemed unable to control himself, and this loss of control is especially interesting in light of the observation mentioned earlier that people today come to psychiatrists because of a lack of impulse control.

Several other recent studies bear on the absence or inaccessibility of the father, and all point to the same conclusions: a father not at home very much contributes to (a) low motivation for achievement, (b) inability to defer immediate gratification for later rewards, (c) low self-esteem, (d) susceptibility to group influence and to juvenile delinquency. The absent father tends to have passive, effeminate, dependent sons lacking in achievement, motivation, and independence. These are general findings with, of course, many exceptions.

So much for current trends that have a greater or lesser effect on all families. What about the future? What can we expect if they continue? First of all, the quality of family life will continue to deteriorate, producing a society with a higher incidence of mental illness than ever before known. Ninety-five percent of our hospital beds will be taken up by mentally ill patients. The nature of this illness will be characterized primarily by a lack of impulse control. In this impulse-ridden society of tomorrow we can expect the assassination of people in authority to be an every-day occurrence. All crimes of violence will increase, even those within the family.

Because battered children -- if they survive -- tend to become parents who, in turn, abuse their children, the amount of violence within the family will increase exponentially.

Aggression turned inward will also increase, and the suicide rate will continue to soar. The greatest number of suicides will continue to be among teenagers and those in mid-life. These two phases of the life cycle have many features in common and perhaps are filled with the greatest stress. In the past twenty years the suicide rate in ten- to fourteen-olds has doubled and in fifteen- to nineteen-year-olds has tripled. The mass suicides we have just witnessed in Guyana may become commonplace.

We will also continue to witness changes in the expression of sexual impulses. We will begin to have a greater understanding of an observation made by Freud over sixty years ago, that when sexual freedom is unrestricted, "love becomes worthless and life empty." As sexuality becomes more unlimited and more separated from family and emotional commitment, the deadening effect experienced will cause more bizarre experimenting and widespread perversion. The signs of the future are quite clear.

Jean O'Leary (a woman appointed by President Carter to serve on the National Commission for the Observance of International Woman's Year) has recently written an article in the *Now* publication. Urging that lesbianism be taught in our schools and requiring school counselors to take courses "to teach a positive view of lesbianism," she writes that students should be encouraged to explore "alternate lifestyles, including lesbianism." And a group in Boston called the Boston Boise Committee have been trying to convince the public that there is nothing "inherently wrong with sex between men and boys," to lower the age of consent to fourteen, and to change the child molestation laws to reduce legal barriers against such relationships.

What can the church do? Here I speak only as a layman.

1. The church, it seems to me, must place greater emphasis on the Christian responsibility of the family. The family consists of relationships, and successful relationships take time and effort and accessibility. The two great commandments make clear that our lives must focus first and foremost on our relationships: first, our relationship with God, and, secondly, our relationship with our neighbor. When Christ was asked, "Who is our neighbor?" He told the story of the Good Samaritan, implying that our neighbor is the first person we come across in need, and since we are all in need, doesn't that include, first and foremost, our family, those who share our home and for whom we have primary responsibility?

Too often, even in the Christian home, we fail to make ourselves accessible, take others for granted, treat children with considerably less respect and common courtesy than we give a visitor. The church needs to teach how the Christian practices *agape* in his moment-by-moment interactions within the family. The Christian home ought to be at least a little more free of the tension and strife and resentment that characterize most families. So often, however, even the minister is so busy taking care of the needs of others,

that he neglects the emotional and spiritual needs of those
for whom he is most responsible.

2. The church must confront directly and become more sophisticated in its understanding of emotional illness. It
must do this if it is to meet the needs of modern society in
the future and if it is to minister effectively to the needs
of its congregation. The evangelical church, it seems to me,
is about forty years behind in its understanding of what modern medicine can do for the emotionally ill. Seminarians
need considerably more background and training in this area.
They need firsthand observation of psychopathology so that
they will be able to recognize when they see it in their pastoral experience and refer people for medical help before it
is too late. A person suffering with an obssessive compul-
sive neurosis who feels that he's committed the unpardonable
sin needs psychiatric treatment before he'll be emotionally
free to draw on the spiritual resources available to him
through his faith. Pastors need to be able to distinguish
between emotional problems and spiritual problems. Though
they are often interrelated, they are not synonymous.

3. The church needs to spell out more clearly Christian
moral values. As a nation, we appear to be more confused
morally than at any time in our history. The church somehow
has failed to give moral leadership to the nation. No clear
voice can be heard.

Perhaps we need to hear a little less about self-fulfillment and a little bit more about self-denial. Perhaps denial
is one key to fulfillment. We need to hear more about the
infinite worth of a human being -- that one child or one
spouse transcends in time and significance all of our secular
institutions put together -- our governments, our universities, and even our institutional churches. Parents often
today resent children because they interfere with their "fulfillment." If a woman of twenty-five has two children, two
years apart, and she gives full time to rearing them until
they are eighteen years old, this leaves her with two-thirds
of her adult life to follow whatever interest she desires.
Is this really too great a sacrifice to ask?

4. I think it would also be helpful for the church to
spell out clearly the Christian sexual ethic. For some reason, the church has been reluctant to speak out clearly on
this issue, and the result has been confusion within many
Christian homes. It's easy to understand this confusion,
especially among young people (though certainly not

exclusively among young people). So many voices in our society point in opposite directions. For a young person to grow up without clear direction in this area imposes enormous stress on him. All of this underscores the need for the church to make its position unmistakably clear.

5. The church ought to play a greater role in curtailing the negative influence of television in the American home. Most damage comes not from those programs that directly attack the Christian faith or Christian standards, but from those that make anti-Christian assumptions and whose attack is latent and indirect. The impact of television on the home is so pervasive and so potentially dangerous that the church cannot afford to ignore it.

6. The church needs to be more aware of legislation that is passed that has a negative influence on the family. The church ought to be alert to and aware of bills that are being considered that are destructive to the family and strongly oppose them. And to support those that will be helpful to the elderly, to children, and to one-parent families.

7. The church needs to realize more fully its enormous potential for healing -- healing especially those specific emotional problems medicine has not been able to deal with effectively. At a research conference on alcoholism in Washington, D.C., Jerome Frank, a professor of psychiatry at Johns Hopkins University, summed up the research findings by pointing out that little had been said about the most consistently effective cure for alcoholism -- namely, religious conversion. And there is evidence of recent research coming out of the University of California where a series of homosexuals, through conversion and through small-group activity within the church, changed from exclusive homosexuality to complete and exclusive heterosexual behavior. The church has a healing ministry that in many areas has only recently begun to be explored.

These are some of the problems of the home as I see them from my perspective and a few suggestions from a very amateur layman of how the church can help meet them.

The Future of the Church:
The Christian Family

Response: Howard G. Hendricks

If the future of the church resides in the family, this paper is telling us we're in trouble. Our work is cut out for us. I heard recently of a young man who was miscast as an angel in the Christmas play. His only line, "Fear not, for behold, I bring you good tidings of great joy," etc. They drilled him, coached him, he reviewed it before his parents, came out on the stage, saw the large group of people and the lights, and his mind went blank. And the only thing he could think of was, "Man, have I got news for you!" That's my conclusion after hearing this paper.

For just a few moments, I would like to share some implications for the church that this paper is not only speaking, but *shouting*, to us. And I'd like to probe five areas of concerted concern that I'll only capsulize -- concerns that ought to provoke, not paralyze, our thinking.

First, this paper is saying to us that the church *must* give higher priority to marriage and the family. We've got to get off the kick that the home exists for the church rather than that the church exists for the home -- that the home is somehow an option rather than an essential. Now, we all give lip-service to this, but in my judgment, we are talking a better game than we are playing. In many cases our churches are doing more to break up our homes than they are to build them up. A prominent pastor in our community recently said to me, "Howie, seventy to eighty-five percent of our families are in trouble." I believe we need to return to the biblical conviction that the home is the primary

teaching-learning environment, and that the church and home
need to work together as a team in cooperation, not in competition. Perhaps we could begin, as several churches have,
in the area of scheduling. I think we've got a moral issue
to face every time we dislodge parents from their homes to
come to church. We need to ask, "Is this trip necessary?"

The *second* thing this paper is saying to me -- and, I
trust, to you -- is that we need to prepare families to cope
with cultural change -- to live in tension. Rather than cap-
itulating to the culture and being conditioned by the culture, make an *impact* upon our culture. Historically, the
church has done better when its opposition is visible and
hostile, and it's done not as well when the opposition from
the culture is unseen and subtle. Several of us were discussing -- we've done a profound job of teaching people worldli-
ness, but with the wrong specifications. We've given people
lists of prohibitions, but the result is that they really do
not know what the *real* world is that is subtly invading their
homes. When Paul said, "Don't allow the world to squeeze you
into its mold," he had a penetrating word to say to the church
in our generation.

Third, this paper is also teaching us that we need to offer
more realistic training for marriage and parenting. We need
to return to the fact that the church must become a school,
a training ground, a resource center for personal development
-- particularly in the family! The church and the home need
to differentiate their roles so that we recognize that the
primary task of the church is training parents; not *doing*
the work of a parent, but *equipping* parents to do the work
that they *alone* can do.

We conclude from this paper, certainly, that the family
doesn't look like we think it looks. I can remember the
shocking frontal attack I got after I wrote a little book
called, *Heaven Help the Home!* I went out to conduct some
family-life seminars, and one day had the courage to ask,
"How many of you are one-parent families?", and I would say
one-third of the audience raised their hands, and I realized
we were speaking in this book to something that did not
exist in over one-third of the homes represented in that
seminar alone! Many of the realities which were pointed out
by this paper are grabbers -- the absent fathers, battered
children, etc.

A *fourth* implication of this paper to us in the church is
that we need to teach greater responsibility and spiritual

resources -- to teach people, "*You* are responsible, but you
are *not* alone. God is interested, and we are interested."
An aggressive return to placing responsibility where it right-
fully belongs; namely, in the home. I'm sure you have seen,
if you are at all involved in the church, that an increasing
number of parents are coming to us to deposit their children
there and saying in effect, "Here, you take the responsibility." And then, when it doesn't turn out, they have someone
to blame. I saw a classic piece of graffitti in Philadelphia
some time ago. Scratched across the wall were these words,
"Humpty Dumpty was pushed!" And I thought, "This is characteristic of a society that is seeking someone to blame."
There is much more that we could say about this, but I think
the paper's attention to our preoccupation with self -- a
form of narcissism that has taken over in our culture -- and
this lack of impulse control certainly directly affects our
teaching of control by the Spirit. But is it control related
to the realistic areas of life to which we were confronted?

Fifth, and last -- and this to me was one of the most exciting features in the paper -- the church must provide
greater exposure to positive role models and a Christian
therapeutic community. We are living in a culture in which
the pedestals are empty, and young people, particularly, are
coming to our schools and to our churches and asking, "What
does a Christian father look like? What does a Christian
mother, wife, etc., look like?" Dr. Harold Voth, distinguished senior psychiatrist and psychoanalyst at the Menninger
Foundation, wrote a book you ought to read, entitled, *The
Castrated Family*. In that book he says, "The cycle of sick
or weak people who are the product of sick or broken families
keeps repeating itself," producing a castrated family.

A number of you, I am sure, were at the Congress on the
Family in St. Louis a few years ago. I still think the most
significant word I heard was by a black pastor from Detroit
who said, "I moved into a community to make an impact for
Jesus Christ, and I began to discover that all the young people who were married in my church were in the process of getting a divorce and were in no way involved in the church."
This led his board to the realization that, "every time we
marry anybody in this church, we take on responsibility for
that marriage." They began a pre-marital counseling program
and a process of adopting couples and farming them out, so
to speak, to older couples who took responsibility for them
for the first three years -- the most determinative years in
a marriage. They began to see the most remarkable and dramatic changes. Hurting people need to be involved with healthy

people, and I believe the church has a profound contribution
to make.

I was in a church not too long ago that's gone to the mini-
church concept. I met that particular night with a small
group that was structured on the basis of an extended family.
There were teenagers, singles, divorced people, couples with
and without children, couples whose children had already
grown, and there were senior citizens. We were meeting in
the home of a woman whose husband has walked out and left her
with three children. She said to me, "Howie, this is the
most exciting thing that's happened in my life! I can hardly
wait for the mini-church to come to our home." In terms of
the impact, the role models -- the older people who are supporting this dear woman in the midst of a crisis -- this is
paydirt!

Maybe this paper is suggesting something rather bold and
radical -- though not verbally stated; namely, if the Billy
Graham Center decides to have another consultation, maybe we
really need a consultation on the *future of the family*.

The Future of the Church: In a Secular Society

Address: Ted Ward

Last year in Atlanta I confessed a deep ambivalence about the future. For society, in general, I see impending tragedy. The probability of catastrophe of one sort or another seems overwhelming. Yet for the church -- for God's people and God's work in the world -- I see great hope. God's resources are limitless; nothing that the church needs to do is hopeless. Even in the presence of secular tragedy and facing the mounting probability of persecution in the church, I am eager to get on with the future. Accounting for one's pessimism while living out one's optimism requires more than psychotherapy; it requires faith;

My commitment to seek God's will for the future was renewed and invigorated last year -- not just as a matter of personal spiritual readiness, but in terms of what the people of God can do that will make a difference in the world until the end. Through this Consultation and similar experiences, many of God's people are finding a more comprehensive and powerful perspective. For example, one of the most recent holistic statements of the contemporary tasks of evangelical Christianity is expressed in the *Willowbank Report*. In it we hear the following:

> We deplore the pessimism which leads some Christians to disapprove of actual cultural engagement in the world and the defeatism which persuades others that they could do no good there anyway and should, therefore, wait in inactivity for Christ to put things right when He comes.

We prefer ... to base the church's cultural responsibility on Scripture rather than history. Our fellow-
men and women are made in God's image, and we are commanded to honor, love, and serve them in every sphere
of life. To this argument from God's creation we add
another from His kingdom which broke into the world
through Jesus Christ. All authority belongs to Christ.
He is Lord of both the universe and church. And He
has sent us into the world to be its salt and light.
As His new community, He expects us to permeate society.

My assignment, to deal with the future relationship of the
evangelical church to the secular society, demands definition
of three terms: future, evangelical church, and secular
society.

First, *Future*. The focus on "intermediate future" is suggested as a delimitation. For most people, the *near* future
is seen as an extension or continuation of what is already
known. "The future" thus tends to be perceived in terms of
today's unsolved problems. On the other hand, the *distant*
future, for most Christians, is perceived in terms of ultimate judgment and/or fulfilled kingdom. Thus, an undesig-
nated use of the term "future" runs into all sorts of ambi-
guity. Is the concern for the future expressed in this Consultation only a matter of coping with the present and anti-
cipating the culmination of the prophecies of the Kingdom of
our Lord? Hardly. It may be all of that, but its uniqueness
lies in grappling with the issues *beyond* the present and
before the culmination. Hence, the term "intermediate future"
is offered in an attempt to clarify this distinction.

Next, *Church*. Defining the church -- or more particularly,
the evangelical sector of the church -- raises *complex* questions. In the interest of getting on with the major burden
of the assignment, a compromise between crisp and foggy definitions is assumed: the church is taken to mean the body of
the redeemed, either within a particular assembly or at large
within a nation, region, or the world. The tasks of the
church include evangelization, and thus Christians hold a
supra-national identity and fellowship in the worldwide mission of the church.

Despite the breadth of the concept *church*, the emphasis of
the paper is on that region of the world in which most of us
recognize our primary stewardship: the church in North America, particularly in the United States and Canada. We cannot
presume to speak for the world.

Finally, the term, *Secular Society* -- a most problematic definition. The distinction between sacred and secular is ancient, but not inherently Christian. In strictest terms, all of life is religious; although the secular society may deny the sacredness of life, the denial comes from spiritual blindness. Indeed, if you hear Willis Harman as I do, the secular sector is now engaged in re-creating the sacred. All of life has theological meaning in the perspective of biblical premises about creation, sin, and judgment.

The totality of human experience is clothed in moral values, and spiritual meanings are embedded in every thought. Nevertheless, the term "secular" is used here in contrast with the godly or the Christian sector.

I. THE SECULAR SOCIETY IN FUTURISTIC PERSPECTIVE

To explore the relationship of evangelical Christianity and secular society in the intermediate future, the place to begin is in the contemporary -- but we dare not be confined to current problems and perspectives. What is the condition of society and of the church today? That's part of it, but the bigger question is: what trend-changing events may be about to emerge?

The systematic study of the future requires the recognition of discontinuity. We now know that any significant new element in the system brings not just more-of-the-same but a whole new set of "rules" whereby social development and history itself are re-conceptualized. Gone is the straight-line notion wherein the future is seen merely as an extension of recent history. *Responsible futurism not only studies trends, but scans the horizon of imagination to identify the possible emergences of factors which will alter everything.*

Secular society is "a mixed bag." The variations within the "secular" sector range from aggressively anti-Christian to warmly sympathetic to Christian values and virtues.

The witness of God in the world, through natural revelation, human conscience, and the continuity of the living Word within His people, has made its mark. The total effect on secular society is undeniably in the direction of morality and spiritual concern, even as defined by secular standards.

The expressions of evil in secular society are widely varied. From time to time and from place to place, "spiritual wickedness in high places" takes various forms: at one

time overt attack on the principles and the people of God;
at another time infiltration and subversion.

The humanistic religiousness of contemporary society is
introspective if not introverted. It speaks of an inner
quest, reflecting the persisting belief that there is little,
if any, responsible authority outside oneself. According to
Robert Elwood in *Alternative Altars*, it is an "increasingly
privatized sort of searching and yet a very intense and very
real searching in all sorts of directions." Looking ahead,
Elwood sees these "religions of feelings" taking two possible
roads. In the face of worldwide hunger and starvation, the
tendency would be toward "doomsday religions." But if somehow human societies muddle through without catastrophe, he
foresees scientific mysticism as the religion of the future.

The secular society seeks piecemeal solutions for basic
human problems. Lacking awareness of the spiritual dimension that ties together all of human traits and functions,
the massive agencies, governmental and private, treat symptoms -- bits and pieces of much larger and more interdependent problems.

If Christians are too inclined to grasp the *spiritual* panacea, it is similarly true that secular people grasp at far
more absurd bits of the whole human dilemma. Technology, especially because of its proven capacity to usher in "brave
new worlds" is seen as the major alternative to moral renewal.

At Harvard last June Solzhenitsyn attempted to scold secular Americans into a moral confrontation with decadence in
society. His attack was broadly aimed at "Western civilization" and its "dangerous trend to worship man and his material
needs." His most specific warning was against humanism's
materialistic tendency:

Even if we are spared destruction by war, our lives will
have to change if we want to save life from self-
destruction. We cannot avoid revising the fundamental
definition of human life and human society. Is it true
that man is above everything? Is there no Superior
Spirit above him? (Solzenhitsyn, 1978).

Among the many who resented this criticism were those who see
humanistic religion as a viable third position:

... Solzhenitsyn's position does not recognize that
some of this nation's most active humanizers also

believe devoutly in God. Many are Jewish, many are
Christian ... the term humanist cannot be equated
with either atheist or materialist ... it is the
humanistic educator who stands as a bulwark against
the cruel and indecent practices promulgated by all
kinds of groups that wish to inhibit the healthful
growth and development of our students. (David Aspy
in *Educational Leadership* [1978]).

Two views of humanism are apparent: *classical* humanism
with its pompous "man is the measure of all things," and
contemporary humanism, in which the moral goodness of man is
expected to bring the ultimate defeat of evil. The latter
view may be even more dangerous than the former; it is un-
testable (short of doomsday) and it exudes a false confidence
born of faith in one's own optimism.

Herman Kahn is popular among the contemporary humanists.
It may be partly because he tells them what they want to
hear. Given enough faith in technology and enough capital
to back up that faith, according to Kahn, it will all come
out just great in the long run. (Note: *in the long run.*)
Kahn's shallowness shows most clearly when he deals with the
next twenty to fifty years and when he skirts the immense
costs of preventing short-run catastrophe.

Most of these problems (energy, unemployment, pollution, food supply, population) in some sense solve
themselves. By solving, I mean you live with them.
I'm really not as optimistic as painted. But I do
think that barring very bad luck or very bad management, we'll have enormous economic progress.

There's no food problem, if you tell me who's
going to pay for it ... (Kahn, in *Sanders*, [1978]).

Technological science is seen as both the oppressor and
the savior. What science has created, science can overcome
-- is the first article of faith for a dominant sector of
secular society. (Some Christians help to nourish that fal-
lacy.) At the same time, some secular analysts are becoming
aware that there are several technological creatures that cannot be brought under control. People are now beginning to
write about a strange and troublesome kink in the yarn.
McCabe describes the sentiments of affluent Americans toward
a future they fear:

Nor do they wish to think about the potential value
and application of technology, it would appear. In
these circumstances, what better than to turn inward,
or to windmills, or to the relatively simple task of
cleaning up, or to nostalgia? Nostalgia is the antidote to fear of what the future might bring. When expectations turn pessimistic, the market in nostalgia
rises. (McCabe, 1978).

Atomic energy and its so-called "peaceful uses" are being
recognized as a monster in our neighborhoods. Even such conservative organs of mass media as *Reader's Digest* is letting
complacent Americans in on a little surprise:

The Nuclear Regulatory Commission, under pressure from
the industry, has allowed serious compromises with
safety to creep into the design, construction, and
operations of U.S. nuclear plants. As a result, the
country has no present way of knowing how safe or un-
safe its nuclear program is. (Miller, 1976).

To walk away and mumble, "I told you so," is irresponsible.
Perhaps as never before, responsible, moral people are needed
in science and technology -- not as slaves of materialism --
to design automobile bodies and attachments for electric hair-
dryers, but on the cutting edge of the scientific counter-
technology committed to bringing the marvels of God's creation back into God-honoring control before they become any
further the tools of intentional, accidental, or negligent
death and destruction.

II. THE SECULARIZATION OF EVANGELICALISM

The catalog of characteristics of the "last days" presented
in II Timothy 3 includes twenty factors. Surely, today's secular society falls under indictment on most of these factors.
But can we face the fact that quite a few church fellowships
and parachurch organizations are vulnerable on many of these
same matters: lovers of self, lovers of money, boastful,
arrogant ... unloving ... malicious gossips ... reckless, con-
ceited, lovers of pleasure more than lovers of God? The dis-
tinctiveness of the Christian community seems threatened by
the process of secularization within itself.

Indeed, perhaps the most insidious form of syncretism
in the world today is the attempt to mix a privatized
gospel of personal forgiveness with a worldly (even
demonic) attitude toward wealth and power. We are

not guiltless in this matter ourselves. (*The Willow-bank Report*, 1978).

The values of the secular society of greatest threat are those that deal with the integrity of the family. The Christian premises of love, fidelity, and responsibility are under deliberate though somewhat subtle attack in the mass media. Television, technology's favorite pet puppy, which, unfortunately, cannot be housebroken, brings into the home an eroding familiarity with lifestyles and values that undercut Christian values, or at least constitute an important dissonance. Remember: people tend to value what they get used to.

The Christian family constitutes a sort of battlefield on which the major secular values wage a continuing battle:

1. *Materialism* affects the Christian family; its ultimate effect is to turn people from a "seeking of the Kingdom of God" to a seeking after the goods of this world through two-paycheck families and neglected children with unsatiated appetites for acquisitions.

2. *Individualism* affects the Christian family; its self-centeredness and selfish ambition retarding development and slowing the maturity of a Christlike focus on service to others.

3. *Faulty communication*, as exemplified in a society wherein knowledge is power, where the senior always talks down to the junior, and where status gives unjust forcefulness to untrue arguments, is a threat to the family. One-way speechmaking substitutes for conversation, and listening becomes the passive role of all but the powerful.

4. *Relativism*, the groundless determination of right and wrong according to whims of the situation, is a deliberate replacement of God's moral authority and His Word. As such, it threatens the Christian family, especially if the family is relying over-much on the church and its programs for the religious education of its children.

5. *Flawed justice* (or lack of concern for justice) is an especially crucial secular value that can affect the Christian home. Might makes right; seniority equals credibility; people deserve what they get -- these are some of the key fallacies of the secular society. The home and the whole church family are to exemplify God's concern for the pursuit of justice.

Thus, the Christian family and the church as a whole are and ought to be in conflict with secular values. But one suspects that many of these secular values may be learned or at least reinforced by experiences in supposedly Bible-based churches, schools, and colleges.

John Perkins has seen relationships among these secular values and describes the recent debilitation, not only of homes, but of the whole evangelical church:

> The purchase of the American Dream, with all of its consumerism and competition and survival mentality, has taken our minds and our resources away from the battleline. The American Dream is keeping us from developing our own leadership and our own economic base from which we can begin to preach the Gospel in our communities

                              * * * *

The comfort culture wins too many times.

                              * * * *

> ... we have cheapened our evangelism to a smile and "Jesus Saves"; we have cheapened our social action to charity or welfare.

Since the secular society has already largely accepted the default of the family, there are millions of children who are not being cared for adequately. (As Professor Nicholi, I also refer to Urie Bronfenbrenner's studies.) Thus something ought to be done -- in the name of concerned humanity. Perhaps it will be necessary to extend public institutions into pre-school child care in the manner of the proposed extended child-care legislation. (Americans do have a long-standing habit of asking schools to fill the gaps resulting from default in any sector of social life.) But if more social welfare mechanisms are created, what will this do to what little is left of the family? By further reducing the importance of the family will we not be formalizing an already sad condition? Should the church fill this gap? Individual churches are rushing into child care and formal schooling at a remarkable pace. To what extent do these efforts reflect Christian values? To what extent are they merely imitations of the secular institutions?

Since the time of Thomas Aquinas, Christianity has been holding hands with Hellenistic-style formal education, largely oblivious of the dangers it poses especially in relation to the development of the church. The dangers are inherent. When the church accepts the schooling model of human development and its assumptions about knowledge, learning, and human relationships, some non-Christian values come along in the bargain. Much that is secular in the church can be traced to its having drawn indiscriminately from the values of the academy of pre-Christian Greece.

The sort of hierarchical and authoritarian leadership that thrives in many evangelical churches should be called what it is: secular. What can be done to encourage the church to withstand secular perversion and to be about its task of confronting culture? ("Secular perversions" here refers to things that are organismic and deeply functional in the church's institutional forms -- violations of justice, truth, responsibility, and unity.) Whatever is secular in its origin and whatever is justified or rationalized by secular and pragmatic logic must be disciplined against the Word and against the reforming work of God in the world. I am fretful not so much about the secular society as about ourselves -- we who are to stand against the worldly order to see that the work of Christ is carried out in the power of the Holy Spirit.

With reference to ecclesiastical leadership styles and hierarchical elitism, the issue is not that the church is confronting some new problem, but that the church historical has never dealt adequately with an *old* problem: Jesus' teaching on servanthood has rarely cut through the institutional structures of historical Christianity.

Many conditions in the church today are reflections of conditions in the secular society. Many people in the church demonstrate the same needs felt by people in the secular society toward their institutions. These very needs -- to be dominated, to be manipulated, to be passive, to "let somebody else do it," and to transfer obligation and responsibility -- are characteristics of today's secular society. The culture of affluent North America has become largely characterized by passivity. To be part of something by simply watching is typical of the secular society. And so it is in many churches.

When the church caters (or panders) to non-Christian needs, the church is on dangerous ground. Consider, for example, these non-Christian needs that are exemplary of fallen humankind: need for status, need for acquisitive individualism, need for being powerful or, by contrast, the need to be dominated by power. These are sick needs; they are unredeemed needs. They are not characteristic of the people of God in any normative, biblical way. Instead, they are secular; yet the church has accepted them as normal.

I observe, with pain, that much of what we stand for as evangelicals looks ever so much like a thorough accommodation to secular norms. Until we get our own house in order it is unlikely that the church's influence on the secular society will be deeply felt.

Holding more firmly to the whole Word of God is the only antidote to the advance of secularism in the church. Christianity is a matter of faith, hope, and love. Not irrational -- and surely not altogether mystical -- Christianity is based on *informed experience*. God has revealed Himself; the message is in our hands to examine, comprehend, implement, and share. Within that message is a substantive view of the future.

III. THE CHALLENGE OF THE SECULAR PERSPECTIVE

The secular world is changing. The church is changing. The ministries of the church, no less than the shaping forces of the world, are changing. At the very least, any adequate way to look at the relationship must deal with change. The important questions are (1) what is happening? and (2) what are the implications for the church? These two questions center on *change*. It is the habit of traditional societies to resist change and thus to avoid change-related questions and, consequently, to develop only minimal competency in dealing constructively with change. When evangelical Christianity in North America reduced the Gospel to a body of propositions about personal salvation, it became a traditional and conservative subculture within an increasingly secular society. The works of God in reformation were delayed.

So much the pity. The desperate here-and-now demands foresight and planning as never before. In a span of less than a century all of humanity has been brought into subjection to petro-chemical technology, the energy for which is now virtually defunct. It is in our time: the oldest among us are only a little younger than the petroleum industry. The single-century doublings of world population became a probability in our lifetime. The conquering of disease and the global proliferation of bio-damage is the mindless trade-off of our lifetime. The wars to end wars and the unthinkable yet probable war to end *life* -- these are of our lifetime.

Where will the thinking and planning come from? Can evangelical Christians rise quickly to the challenge of the times? Can they learn to do, belatedly, what the evangelical subculture has previously discouraged -- to think and plan for the intermediate future?

The Christian's faith is not taken seriously if it is only a mechanical preoccupation, fixated on the mechanics and chronology of rapture and tribulation. Faith that refuses to be addressed to the realities of our troubled times is not worth having. In the perceptions of secular scholarship, the Christian -- especially the evangelical -- is still lumped with the primitive Bible-thumper as largely "out of it." Christianity is not seen as offering any promising answers; surely the church (no matter what theological color) is not seen as a powerful force. The stereotype is still being reinforced by the sweet, benevolent, entertaining (and mindless) glimpses of Christian community now offered on late-night television. Instead of coming to grips with the screams of a society that is steadily becoming more conscious of its sure destiny, the pulpits drone on and on with that perversion of eternal security that sounds ever so much like complacent singing in a very distant lifeboat.

Christians have lost the initiative on many of the pressing social issues. Instead of having an agenda of redemptive themes, evangelical Christianity is seen often as being a one-issue movement. Listen to this:

To be for freedom, justice, and peace in America today is to speak against war and imperialism, against racism and witch-hunts, against corporate monopoly and tax rip-offs and economic exploitation.

The paragraph above seems almost to be the outline for a Twentieth-Century version of the Magnificat! But, no, it is merely an advertisement for a radical magazine called *The Progressive*.

Perhaps these words seem less important, less convincing to the Christian who knows they come from secular humanists; but the message must be taken seriously. Christians must become brave enough to hold onto biblical principles and biblical language even when they are co-opted or reflected from secular sources. Why should we be less enthusiastic about liberation, justice, peace, unity, and dialogue simply because these have become catchwords of various secular or quasi-Christian movements?

IV. METAPHORS FOR THE INTERMEDIATE FUTURE

Students of the Bible are quite familiar with two rudi-
mentary metaphors of the function of the church in the world:
salt and light.

"Ye are the salt of the earth ..." The disciples of Jesus
Christ are thus described in terms of an active process of
involvement. The oft-rehearsed function of salt in preservation and forestalling decay says much about the worth of the
church in the world. To the Jewish listeners on that moun-
tainside, *salt* would also have suggested wisdom -- the need
to be informed and to apply knowledge. Salt would have suggested perpetuity and covenant -- the symbols are of God's
faithfulness to His people and through His people to the
needs of the whole world. Further, the symbolic meaning of
salt was associated with hospitality. Commissioning His
disciples to be salt provided a metaphor of their serving in
the world and thus extending God's invitation to care and
sustenance.

The major thrust of Christ's use of the metaphor should
not be overlooked: " ... but if the salt have lost his savour
wherewith shall it be salted? It is thenceforth good for nothing ..." The message includes the admonition not to be content with the designation -- the label -- as salt, but to be
about the business of *being* salt.

"Ye are the light of the world." In this second rudiment-
ary metaphor Jesus shares a symbol that is part of His own
being and is included in the descriptions and the self-
descriptions of Christ. Identified in the first creative
process (Genesis 1:3), symbolic of joy, encouragement, new
hope, spiritual comfort, and authorship of enlightenment,
light is a powerful metaphor. Fulfillment of this metaphor
implies visibility and assertiveness.

In theological perspective, the metaphor of light speaks
of identifying with Christ in that redemptive process of the
Gospel, bringing spiritual enlightenment and awakening moral
consciousness, enabling secular humankind to see themselves
more clearly and to bring their works into judgment under the
righteousness of God. The major vehicle is the "good works"
which become visible because the Christian's reflection of
Christ illuminates them. These good works are not of the
Christian's doing except as the Holy Spirit brings them about
as His own fruit: love, joy, peace, longsuffering, gentle-
ness, goodness, faith, meekness, and temperance.

In these two metaphors we have a detailed picture of the
work of the church in the world. Whatever the future may
bring, these metaphors will stand. All our images of the
future -- and especially our images of the future of the
church -- start here.

We must choose well the path to walk into the future.
Alternative metaphors can be the starting point for an ex-
ploratory study of the choices open to us in the probable
conditions of the intermediate future. I offer four:

Metaphor I -- The Unheeded Conscience

If Herman Kahn and others who foresee a rosy future fulfilled through wonders of science and technology are right,
the church is likely to be all but forgotten. If evidences
of long-term resolutions of the dominant human social problems (hunger, disease, political oppression, and war) do appear, Christians should readily thank God for yet another re-
prieve for sinful humankind. But with the passage of time
-- especially of an *easy* time -- the "light of the world"
will be less and less welcome. In the minds of many the
question would be (far more than today) "Who needs it?" The
Church of Jesus Christ, as holder of the testimony of God's
truth, would be seen as superfluous -- good times produce
less God-consciousness than do foxholes. Thus the church --
the *unheeded conscience* -- may itself lapse into profound
neglect or apostasy.

Metaphor II -- The Ghetto

Minorities of various sorts, particularly religious and
racial, have been pushed into ghettos. Throughout history,
minorities which posed psychic threat to those in the ascen-
dancy were enslaved or oppressed. In the Middle Ages the
term *ghetto* described the place where a minority population
chose to live (or was required to live) -- a distinct and
peculiar people in an assigned place within a larger society.
Christians should take special note that the institutionalization of the ghetto, in Europe and much later in the United
States, was to keep God's ancient people, the Jews, "in their
place."

It can happen again -- especially if conditions become
very bad and a scapegoat is needed (as in Nazi Germany). To
mobilize and encourage the ascendant society, some minority
may once again be singled out for "special treatment." In
order to qualify for this dubious benefit, a group of people

must be indeed distinct. They must either dress differently,
look different, believe differently, or have very different
customs. Preferably, there should be at least a bit of truth
in the accusation that they see themselves as being superior
in some way that is irritating or offensive to the large
society. So long as evangelical Christians are mostly white,
middle-class, aspiring, acquisitive winners in the capital-
istic game of secular society, they are unlikely to qualify
as unique except in their self-proclaimed pietisms.

But in the highly probable event that the value system of
the church will become more clear and more firm and, because
of the increasingly worldly values of the secular society,
the church will come more directly into confrontation, the
conditions for persecution will have been met. From then on
it will be only a matter of time and a question of intensity.
The church of Jesus Christ will once again come under sustained and systematic persecution. The community of the family of God may be invited, encouraged, or even compelled to
keep to itself. The church as the ghetto of godly influence
-- isolated -- its effect as salt and light effectively
neutralized.

Through their experiences during the Holocaust of Nazi occupation, the Polish Jews learned something very curious
about themselves and their ghettos. To be forced into isolation, people have to have or come to accept a "ghetto
mentality." They have to come to see being isolated and
being cut off from the ascendant society as being somehow
appropriate or deserved.

Today "ghetto mentality" has come to mean that lack of
self-esteem that makes a person or group particularly vulnerable to being persecuted. No discredit to the faithful,
brave Jewish people, but to understand modern Israel, one
must see it as the place where many of the survivors of
Hitler's horrors apply today what they learned in the ghettos.
The cry, "never again," rings out, inspiring a sense of identity, of purpose, and, consequently, of worth. "They may kill
us. But we will not be herded into submission."

Since the church in modern times has had no large-scale
experience with the demeaning effects of the ghetto, Christians may do even as the Jews did in the early middle ages;
create their own ghettos, voluntarily, as a misguided investment in group security.

When the principle of love is brought to bear as an evaluative criterion, the ghetto falls short. The ghetto speaks of a hope for saving oneself and one's own. But the cost is relinquishing the contacts through which the church ministers to a spiritually dying secular society. God never meant for His people to accept the ghetto mentality.

Metaphor III -- The Underground

The *underground* suggests a necessity to achieve principled objectives in concealed, covert, or extra-legal ways. In the period when the United States was developing a moral conscience in reference to slavery, the "Underground Railroad" was an only slightly organized network of godly and humanitarian people working together to help slaves gain freedom in the free states or in Canada.

The broader use of the term underground is in reference to resistance or guerrilla movements within an invaded or occupied country. There is something romantic, almost rhapsodic, in the courage and persistence of a resistance fighter in the underground. His or her head is unbowed. To live is for honor, to die is greater honor. While the underground lives, the enemy's victory is hollow. If the underground dies, hope dies with it.

This is our Father's world. We claim it in His name for the furtherance of His redemptive works. But it has been invaded. The enemy occupies our Father's world. The church, if not highly visible, is at least present in the form of an underground resistance. The victory of Satan is hollow, so long as this underground lives. And it will live; our Lord promises, " ... I will build my church."

The likelihood of increased tension between the church and the secular society raises the question of persecution. After centuries of drifting with the secular tide, the church can hardly go any further; even the one crucial issue of family values (love, fidelity, and responsibility) may differentiate Christians as a peculiar minority. The maintaining of a godly lifestyle in the face of increasing secularism, especially since that secularism is destined to be materialistic and spiritually empty, will fulfill all the prime conditions for persecution. Persecution, coupled with increased anxiety over the spiritual integrity of our families, could easily force Christians underground. A minority, persecuted, fearful, but surviving as the witness of God in a perverse era.

Again, from John Perkins,

> The world is tiring, but we are to endure. The
> world will become frustrated, but we can have hope.
> The world will withdraw, but we must strike. We are
> God's guerrilla fighters, his spiritual saboteurs.
> We must now go to battle in our communities armed
> with the evangelism, social action, and political
> encounter through which Jesus can work. (Perkins,
> 1975).

The underground metaphor has one major problem. It is
drawn from the experiences of warfare (a not unfamiliar nor
unbiblical frame of reference for "soldiers of the cross" who
are armed with the armor, the shield, and the sword). But the
watchword of any underground is "kill or be killed." The
Christian commitment to love our enemies and to pray even for
those who despitefully use us requires a most unusual sort
of an underground. If the metaphor is apt at all, it suggests a process to subvert secularism through love, concern,
and good works, fulfilled as "insiders" or infiltrators.

If Christians reject being pushed into a ghetto and are
able to avoid the paranoia that can undermine an effective
underground, the conditions are just right for fulfilling
this metaphor. Those of us who work within the institutions
of secular society are aware just how well God has distri-
buted His faithful. It is not just recently that Christians
are holding strategic roles in government, institutional education, health care, media, and other influential public sectors. Wherever one turns, it is reassuring to discover that
God has His witness. We are a distinct minority, for sure,
but we are there, fulfilling the preservative and curative
functions of the "salt of the earth." In recent years the
trend has been for these infiltrators to take their mission
more seriously and to differentiate more firmly between good
and evil, speaking up more boldly, acting more on faith and
accepting less of the pragmatism that undermines godliness.

Indeed, the church as a bold and brave underground is an
apt metaphor if we are to seek a recapturing -- a possessing
-- of the secular world in the name of Jesus Christ.

Metaphor IV -- The Field Hospital

The world is at war. Literally and figuratively, "wars
and rumors of wars" have long characterized the human condition. But the warfare of guns, armaments, and the military

is only the visible tip of deeper trauma. Spiritual warfare constantly affects all humankind. "For we wrestle not against flesh and blood, but against principalities, against powers, against the rulers of the darkness, against spiritual wickedness in high places" (Ephesians 6:12). This warfare is not only a matter of the forces of God against the forces of Satan. Indeed, such is the evil that besets this world that it knows no peace within itself. The "peace that passes all understanding" is inner peace, not freedom from external attack and conflict. The secular world does not have inner peace. People of the secular society are constantly victimized *by each other* and by the inescapable pressures, anxieties, doubts, infidelities, and passions that dominate the unredeemed creation. Satan hates the church, but he treats his own people hatefully, all the same.

The spiritual *warfare* among secular people shows every promise of increasing. As the secular society seeks freedom without responsibility, truth without source, and "the good life" without justice, degeneration will mount to hysterical trauma. The casualities of this warfare are already piling up; one can hardly imagine the suffering to come. Will we prepare ourselves to staff the *field hospitals*? The Christian community, although resented for its peculiarity, may very well be appreciated for its healing and restorative capabilities.

It is in the redeemed nature to be engaged in the relief of human suffering and to be active in constructive and restorative processes. Evangelical Christianity shows signs of moving away from its defensiveness, its obsessive self-demonstration, and its self-righteous weighing out of each good act according to its "opportunity" to serve as a vehicle for verbal witness. We may be returning to the heart of Christ's compassion wherein the motive of good works is not clever strategy but an expression of what we *are*.

The field hospital is more than a tent and a stack of medical supplies. What makes it work is people who know what they are doing. Among the proposed metaphors of the church in the intermediate future, the *field hospital* demands the most in the way of preparation. The gifts of the Holy Spirit to the church must be claimed not only for the good of our own inside community, but also for our servanthood in the secular society. To fulfill the ministry of Christ to a needy world we must claim the gifts of healings and helps. It may well be the destiny of the church to minister in the front lines among the spiritual, emotional, and physical traumas

that fall out from the culmination of the power of Satan.
The church may honor its Lord best as the field hospital --
a prepared community of relief and restoration in tragic
times.

I close with a reminder from the *Lausanne Covenant*:

... we affirm that evangelism and socio-political involvement are both part of our Christian duty. For
both are necessary expressions of our doctrines of God
and man, our love for our neighbor and our obedience
to Jesus Christ. The message of salvation implies a
message of judgment upon every form of alienation,
oppression and discrimination, and we should not be
afraid to denounce evil and injustice wherever they
exist. When people receive Christ they are born
again into his kingdom and must seek not only to
exhibit but also to spread its righteousness in the
midst of an unrighteous world. The salvation we
claim should be transforming us in the totality of
our personal and social responsibilities. Faith
without works is dead.

REFERENCES

Aspy, David N.   "A Humanist Answer to Alexander Solzhenitzyn." *Educational Leadership*. Vol. 36, No. 1, (October, 1978).

Baier, Kurt, and Rescher, Nicholas. *Values and the Future.* (New York: Free Press, 1969).

Bibby, Reginald W.   "Why Conservative Churches Really Are Growing: Kelley Revisited." *Journal for the Scientific Study of Religion*.   (June, 1978).

Brown, Lester R.   *The Twenty-Ninth Day*.   (New York: W. W. Norton, 1978).

Cassidy, Richard J.   *Jesus, Politics, and Society*. (Maryknoll, N. Y.:   Orbis Books, 1978).

Cerling, C.E., Jr.   "Some Guidelines for Evangelical Involvement." *Evangelical Newsletter*, Vol. 5, No. 19 (September 22, 1978).

Collins, Gary R.   *Our Society in Turmoil*.   (Carol Stream: Creation House, 1970).

Cox, Harvey.   *The Secular City: Secularization and Urbanization in Theological Perspective*.   (New York: Macmillan, 1965).

Douglas, J.D., ed.   *Let the Earth Hear His Voice*. (Minneapolis: World Wide Press, 1975).

Ellwood, Robert.   *Alternative Altars*.   (In press).

Ellul, Jacques.   *The Presence of the Kingdom*. (Philadelphia: Westminster Press, 1951).

Grounds, Vernon C.   *Revolution and the Christian Faith*. (Philadelphia: Holman/Lippincott, 1971).

Hall, Thor.   *The Future Shape of Preaching*.   (Philadelphia: Fortress Press, 1971).

Henry, Carl.   "Evangelical Profits and Losses." *The Christian Century*.   (January 25, 1978).

Hitt, Russell T. "Approaching the Bi-Millenial."
Evangelical Newsletter. Vol. 2, No. 9 (October, 1975).

Hoke, Donald. *Evangelicals Face The Future*. (South
Pasadena: William Carey Library, 1978).

Holmes, Urban T., III. *The Future Shape of Ministry*.
(New York: Seabury Press, 1971).

Humanist Manifestos I and II. (Buffalo: Prometheus Books,
1973).

Kenniston, Kenneth. *All Our Children -- The American
Family Under Pressure*. (New York: Harcourt Brace
Jovanovich, 1977).

Knoll, Erwin, and Postol, Theodore A. "The Day The Bombs
Went Off." *The Progressive*. (October 1978).

Lausanne Committee for World Evangelization. *The
Willowbank Report -- Gospel and Culture*. (Wheaton:
Lausanne Committee..., 1978).

Lens, Sidney. "The Doomsday Strategy." *The Progressive*.
(February, 1976).

Lockberbie, Bruce. *The Cosmic Center*. (Grand Rapids:
Eerdmans, 1977).

Marshall, I. Howard. "Slippery Words." *Expository Times*.
(June, 1978).

Marty, Martin E. *The Search for A Usable Future*. (New
York: Harper and Row, 1969).

McCabe, Peter. "The Sound of Doom." *Harper's*.
(February, 1978).

Miller, James Nathan. "The Burning Question of Brown's
Ferry." *Reader's Digest*. (April, 1976).

Northcross, Mark. "Who Will Own the Sun?" *The
Progressive*. (April, 1976).

Parker, Everett, and Jennings, Ralph. "Turning the Public
Out." *Christianity and Crisis*. (July 17, 1978).

Perkins, John. "A Strategy for Change." *Post American*. (June-July, 1975).

Peters, Ted. *Futures -- Human and Divine*. (Atlanta: John Knox Press, 1978).

Prior, Kenneth F. W. *The Gospel in a Pagan Society*. (Downers Grove: Inter-Varsity Press, 1975).

Sanders, Kevin, moderator. "Kahn, Mead, and Thompson: A Three-Way Debate on the Future." (Herman K., Margaret M. and William Irwin T.) *The Futurist*. Vol. XII, No. 4 (August, 1978).

Schaeffer, Francis A. *The Church at the End of the 20th Century*. (Downers Grove: Inter-Varsity Press, 1970).

Sider, Ronald J. *Rich Christians in an Age of Hunger*. (Downers Grove: Inter-Varsity Press, 1977).

Sider, Ronald J. "The Christian College: Beachhead or Bulwark." *The Other Side*. (August, 1978).

Smith, Ronald Gregor. *The Whole Man*. (Philadelphia: Westminster Press, 1969).

Solzhenitzyn, Alexander. Commencement Address, Harvard University, June 10, 1978.

Sontag, Susan. "The Imagination of Disaster." *Mass Media and Mass Man*. Alan Casty, ed. (New York: Holt, Rinehart and Winston, 1968).

Stott, John. *The Lausanne Covenant, An Exposition and Commentary*. (Minneapolis: World Wide Publications, 1975).

Ward, Ted. *The Influence of Secular Institutions on Today's Family*. (Omaha: Family Concern, Inc., 1975).

Ward, Ted. "The Christian's Family in Society" in *Living and Growing Together*. Gary R. Collins, ed. (Waco: Word Books, 1976).

Weaver, James H. and Wisman, Jon D. "Smith, Marx, and Malthus -- Ghosts Who Haunt Our Future." *The Futurist*. Vol. XII, No. 2. (April, 1978).

Wren, Brian. *Education for Justice.* (Maryknoll, N.Y.: Orbis Books, 1977).

In respect and appreciation for those now indispensable review services that direct the attention to valuable and scattered resources, the four which the author reads regularly are cited following:

Evangelical Newsletter. William J. Petersen, Editor, with Robert W. Patterson, Russell T. Hitt, George C. Fuller. 1716 Spruce St., Philadelphia, PA 19103.

Sources & Resources. Youth Specialities, 861 Sixth Avenue, San Diego, CA 92101.

Public Justice Newsletter. APJ Education Fund, Box 5769, Washington, D.C. 20014.

Scan. Robert T. Coote, Editor, with Susan B. Krass. Partnership in Mission, 1564 Edgehill Rd., Abington, PA 19001.

The Future of the Church: In a Secular Society

Response: John M. Perkins

I am really delighted to be at this conference. It is a pleasure to have this opportunity to respond to Dr. Ted Ward's speech. I have had opportunity to study it and appreciated it so very much.

Last year I went to Atlanta, but due to illness I didn't get a chance to really enjoy the conference. I am thrilled with the possibility of the kind of light that can come within the evangelical church from this kind of conference. I am also excited about what the evangelical church could do in terms of implementing some of the vision from a conference like this.

I come to you with the freshness of my own conversion experience. I am not from a Christian background, so it is a transforming experience and thrilling to me to know Christ as Savior. It was through my son that I met Christ when I was twenty-seven years old, and it is still a thrill.

I come, believing that we can really make a difference in society if we really take the Word of God seriously and if we really try to flesh out the Gospel of Jesus Christ. I come *living for the future*. Anyone living in Mississippi through the sixties had to look to the future. We could not look at the present; we had to look to the future. I am always looking to the future and hoping for a better day. So, I am delighted to be here to talk about the future of the church in a secular society.

What I think has happened to the church and what I heard
Dr. Ward saying in his speech, is that the church -- the evangelical church in particular -- has really lost its identity
in the world. We have lost that sense of being pilgrimage
people. We have become merged into the world despite Paul's
admonition when he says, "Be not conformed to this world, but
be ye transformed by the renewing of your mind, that ye may
prove what is that good and acceptable and perfect will of
God." I believe we are really lost when we have lost our
identity. But I believe the Spirit of God is trying to give
us a sense of what it means to be the people of God in our
world today. We are trying to *claim* our identity, and so I
see coming together at this conference as an attempt for us
as evangelicals to try to gain our identity here in the world.

I remember when the Billy Graham Crusade was to be held in
Jackson in 1975. This was a blessing to us in Mississippi.
Dr. Graham had said that he would not hold a crusade in
Mississippi unless the church worked together in a cross-
fertilization of blacks and whites. It was a thrill and a
new opportunity to test this "new South." We met together
at the Holiday Inn to talk about the plans for the crusade,
and they wanted me and a lot of other blacks within the city
to be on the steering committee.

So we met together and began to talk and discuss what the
crusade was going to be like in Mississippi. Then after a
long discussion, I got up and said something that didn't
sound very good. I said to them, "I'm really thrilled with
Dr. Graham's coming to Jackson, Mississippi. I think it's a
wonderful opportunity for us as the people of Mississippi and
of Jackson. I don't know whether or not I am in a position
or whether or not I really want to participate in making
Christians like the ones we have made in the past because the
Christians we have had in the past have been my problem!"

I went on to explain that to them. I said,

Because of having paid the price we have paid and
going through what we have gone through to claim our
identity of evangelical ministry here in Mississippi,
I don't know if I am ready to sell myself out too
cheaply with you people.

What is going to happen is that each night I will
be sitting on the platform, and when Dr. Graham speaks,
there will be thousands of people who are going to come
down and to receive Christ and make a commitment to

faith in Jesus Christ. Those young people -- those young black people -- are going to see me sitting there, and they are going to believe that I agree with all of this. Then some of them are going to go into some of your churches and be turned away. I don't know whether I want to make that kind of Christian.

We had a long discussion out of that. But what happened? Last Christmas my assistant, a black Haitian, was turned away from a 3,000-member Baptist church just five blocks down the street from me. Two months ago my only grandchild was turned away from a day-care center of a 3,000-member Baptist church down the street on the other side. So, when I come to this kind of meeting, I come wondering whether or not we are going to *examine the quality of the believers* that are converted to Jesus Christ. Each of us needs to begin to examine that. I think what we have to do is find our identity as the people of God. We must be the people of God -- called out of the world and called into a relationship with Jesus Christ to be His people, His body. As the people of God we become *His replacement on earth* in community with His people. That is what the church was supposed to be. It was supposed to be the people of God, the body of Christ, *living out the life of Jesus Christ* in the local community.

What we are supposed to do is to have a holistic view of the Gospel. I always say that there is one thing about the evangelical church: the evangelical church has learned how to rightly divide the Word of Truth, but we can't put it back together and preach it in a holistic way in the sense that God intended it. What we need to preach then is the holistic Gospel -- a Gospel that includes social and political involvement in society. We must learn the *purpose of the Gospel*. Where I come from in Mississippi, we don't even know the purpose of the Gospel.

Sometimes, when I go around the country and speak, I put the Mississippi people in a difficult position. In their effort to create a new image for themselves, they are forced to identify with me and accept me because people in other parts of the country have. When we are together, they have to say something, but they become defensive. They say, "Well, Brother John, you talk about reconciliation. You talk about the people of God in a body who will be living out that life in Jesus Christ together. But we put our emphasis on other things. We put our emphasis on evangelism, on church buildings, and structure."

I say, "You put your emphasis in the wrong place. The emphasis and the purpose of the Gospel is to reconcile people together and to reconcile them together in one body. That's the *purpose* of the Gospel. And in the body of Jesus Christ there was not supposed to be Jew nor Gentile, but we are supposed to be one in Jesus Christ." The intention of the Gospel is to reconcile people together. God was in Christ, reconciling the world to Himself, and He has given us the ministry of reconciliation.

I believe the homogeneous idea is really just confirming the condition we are in. It tries to give credibility to the condition we have in the church. The purpose of the Gospel is to call men out of the world and to call them into a fellowship, into a body. The church must show the world they are Christians because they are living out their lives and loving each other in that body. We are cheapening our Gospel. We have "a form of godliness but deny the power of God."

I submit that I really heard Dr. Ward saying three things about the future of the church:

The *first* thing is that the church is going to have to *claim* its identity.

Then, it is going to have to *relocate* itself. We need to have a new concept of mission. The church is going to have to become the body of Christ in the area of need. Instead of us just trying to win people programmatically, we have to become the people of God in the community of need. Suburban churches have to send teams of people back into the area of need and make the Gospel come alive there. We have to believe the Gospel can reconcile; that is the purpose of the Gospel. If you don't believe the Gospel can reconcile, don't preach it! We must believe the Gospel can reconcile.

The *last* thing we have to do is *to model a whole new redistribution system* within the world. The problem I see in all areas of need is the problem of technology and skills. It is not that we don't have the ability to produce doctors and lawyers and the best people in the world. The problem is that we can't get those people to the area of need. We are facing today a problem of redistribution of goods and services to the areas of need.

If we are to meet the challenges facing the church, we have to be *motivated more*. *We have to be motivated by the love of Jesus Christ!*

The Future of the Church: The Essential Components of World Evangelization

Address: Ralph D. Winter

I've been reading the book of Mark recently and have been struck by the fact that *both* the disciples and Jesus were very interested in the future, but that they had *distinctly different agendas*. Probably the most shocking collision of concerns was when James and John waited impatiently for Jesus to finish his awesome prediction detailing his impending arrest, torture, and execution, and then they immediately popped the burning question deriving from their own agenda, expressing their strong concern for their own security. Their small, reasonable -- but very human request to sit on His right hand and His left hand -- totally ignored what Jesus had just told them. Nowhere in the world's literature can you point out so stunning a non sequitur.

The discrepancy between the disciples' perspective on the future and that of our Lord is also seen in their final gathering together with Him in an upper room before His death. With one accord they all vowed they would remain true to Him. But when the going got rough only a few hours later, with equal unanimity they all turned tail and fled.

Even after the resurrection and following His impressive reiteration to them of the Great Commission -- laying on them the obligation of reaching to the ends of the earth -- their agenda was *still* significantly different. In Acts 1:6 their own agenda again surfaces: "Lord, are you *now* going to free Israel from Rome and restore our country as an independent nation?" Jesus, in His reply in Acts 1:8, sidestepped their patriotic concern, their nationalism, their basically self-

directed thinking, by simply restating once more God's un-
changing and decisively larger concern for all other human
societies, and by explaining further that the coming of the
Holy Spirit would endue them with a new and different power
-- and evidently a *new* and *different perspective* to go with
that power.

The remainder of the book of Acts and the following 1,946
years bringing us to the threshold of 1979 bear out this prediction in a mixed pattern. The disciples had to be *driven*
out of Jerusalem by persecution. The Gothic tribal peoples
-- called *Barbarians* by the Romans -- heard the Gospel not
from deliberately commissioned missionaries but from exiled
bishops who had a defective Christology.

Later, the people still further north, the Vikings, yielded
to the Gospel -- to a great extent through the witness of
Christian girls they took captive on their murderous raids
into a by-then settled, complacent, wealthy Christendom in
the British Isles and southern Europe.

Still later, considerable numbers of both Barbarians and
Vikings pulled clear from the yoke of Rome in what we fondly
call the *Reformation*, but patriotic and nationalistic preoc-
cupations busied the Protestants for over two hundred years
before even a tiny trickle of them rediscovered the Great Commission in their treasured vernacular Bibles and yielded to
God's supra-national agenda.

*It was not until the evangelicals appeared in the Protest-
ant stream (200 years after Luther) that any serious attention by Protestants was given to the most prominent mandate
in the Bible.* Even then, when William Carey published a
little book which was to become probably the most influential
document outside of the Bible itself leading to the fulfillment of the Great Commission, he represented a very distinct
minority. In view of the typical divergence between even the
evangelical agenda and the biblical agenda, it is not sur-
prising that you can visit 5,000 Christian bookstores in the
U.S. and not find a single copy of that strategic work available for sale.

These hints from biblical and historical sources must
surely lead us to certain monumental cautions as we look into
the future. It is a tribute to the organizing committee of
this conference that world evangelization even comes into the
agenda. But as we consider the future of the church, we may
do well to recognize what seems to be the consistent thrust

of the whole Bible -- that *unless and until, in faith, the future of the world becomes more important than the future of the church, the church has no future.* As Jesus stated, the most dangerous thing you can do is to seek to save your own life. It is not merely a curiosity, noted by Archbishop Temple (who in his youth was one of the ushers at the 1910 World Missionary Conference),that the Christian church is the only human society that exists exclusively for the purpose of benefitting those outside its membership. This fact is not a curiosity, but a way of life that is *the* way *to* life -- for others and for us.

Thus, to turn it around backwards, world evangelization is the *only* future of the church. Every church in history that has not reached out has gone down. Couple this fact with the logical statement that "unto whomsoever much is given, of him shall much be required" and world evangelization is no longer an option in which the super-zealous can gain extra "brownie points." It suddenly appears to be (and must actually become) the central and fundamental concern of the evangelical move-ent if there is any future for that movement.

Only twice in this century have the people of our country been faced with an overwhelming emergency call -- upon our manhood, our resources, and our civilian population. World War I drew in my father. My older brother and I got caught in the latter stages of World II. My children barely missed out on the Vietnam War, but only a relatively small part of our population (one out of 400 at the peak) ever participated in that war, and my own college young people live and move in a generation that is, for the most part, open, eager, willing to be useful.

Let me return to my own generation. My father is now long retired, out of power. My children do not yet control major social forces. It is *our* generation that followed men like Patton, Eisenhower, MacArthur, Nimitz, to the ends of the earth, and then came back and in just twenty years jerked this nation from a post-depression poverty gulch into what is still (well, barely) the world's most greedy, powerful, and benevo-lent nation. At this conference I am mainly addressing my own generation. It is the one I know best. *It is the generation that now still clearly controls America and will still be in control until about 1984.* Harry Truman was the last of the First World War presidents. From then on, all are World War II veterans -- Eisenhower, Kennedy, Johnson, Nixon, Ford, and Carter. The presidential election of 1984 may well be the watershed of power of the Second World War generation.

In these terms, the mood, the perspective, the brains, the hopes of my generation have only one more full presidential term to run. In this sense this group here assembled has just five more years to exert its primary leadership. We can talk all we want about what others ought to do, who are older or younger. We cannot -- we must not -- avoid the tough questions facing us and our immediate followers!

When our time of direct, decision-making leadership runs out, will the decisions we make now commend themselves to the younger generation? Will the lifestyle we have created and enjoyed be good enough -- or perhaps *too* good -- for those that follow us? Will our vision be profound enough to attract the backing and enable the continuity that only a next generation can provide? Will the deeds we do measure up at least to *God's* expectation of us? Note, if somehow we cannot count on our undertaking to carry over to our children, the resulting hiatus will be a grave discontinuity -- the breaking of the backbone, if you wish -- in the body of our nation's long-term potential in God's purposes.

Now, as I see it, the crux of the matter is in evangelical hands, and the very edge of the edge is the matter of how we evangelicals will respond to the clearest and most central mandate of the Bible: the Great Commission.

You'll say, "Aren't we doing OK?" Frankly, world evangelization as a practical, feasible goal is now only a marginal concern among American evangelicals of my generation. It wouldn't have to be. It ought not to be. But it is! *Last year at this time we were all so scared out of our wits by future talk that our scenarios barely stuttered out a few brave words about world evangelism.* This year we can very easily succumb for various reasons to a marginalized concept of world evangelization, giving lip service to what we no longer believe. Oh, no one here would deny the validity of the Great Commission. It is just that our youthful recklessness in the Second World War is a long way behind us. Our derring-do in science and industry is now jaded by the environmental and energy crises. We are now getting what rest we can, on our laurels. Candidly, we are not at this point prepared psychologically, intellectually, or spiritually, for any kind of a major new forward move across a needy and tumultuous world. What relative security we have makes all dangers look larger. Our young people, much more eager to go than we are, await our leadership. Can we let them down? Can we, in our last five years in control, ask God to give us new and final

resolve so that we can go on into our sixties and seventies
satisfied that we did not give up too soon?

I do believe God is leading us, *our generation*, to new
hope, new faith, to *attempt* great new things for God and to
expect great new things from God. He is certainly working
among our children, by a major, unprecedented moving of God's
Spirit, highlighted in Lausanne and reflected by the bright
new bravery of the Urbana youth -- 8 percent in 1970, 28 percent in 1973, and 51 percent in 1976 -- who signed those cards
laying their lives in God's hands. Can we betray and defeat
this as-yet-undaunted courage? Yes, we can. Easily! So
easily! All we have to do is glance away from the heavenly
vision, lose our nerve *now*, after all we've done -- shift our
feet instead of boldly striding forward. We can at this point
much more easily abdicate than lead. But if we do, we will
desperately, desperately regret it!

Other men, at other times, have given every ounce of their
energies not only to do battle with the forces of evil but
also to strain forward to fulfill God's highest with their
utmost. The list in Hebrews eleven no longer need stop there.
The early Christians gave up their lives in the arenas of
Rome. The converted Germanic tribal peoples gave over their
faith to the savage, invading Vikings. Those Vikings, once
converted, have been ambassadors to the ends of the earth.

But reaching out has not been automatic nor easily achieved.
It took Protestants (with their newly translated vernacular
Bibles) over 200 years before the Great Commission began to
speak through to them. Finally, in 1792 William Carey published something like a lawyer's brief, insisting on the
authority and significance of the Great Commission. Thanks
to the Evangelical Awakening, which brought a greening spring
to all England for the previous quarter of a century, and
thanks to Captain Cook, who proved literally that Britain's
newly won freedom of the seas would readily allow English-
speaking missionaries to go to to the ends of the earth, by,
say, 1825, Protestants could begin to claim that they were
giving at least minor attention to the Great Commission.

Those first efforts were immeasurably strengthened and expanded due to the revival period ranging from Finney to Moody,
and a second major force then emerged in the form of the faith
mission movement, sparked now not by William Carey, but by J.
Hudson Taylor, for whom the left-out peoples were preeminent.
His China Inland Mission was joined by the Sudan Interior Mission, the Africa Inland Mission, the Heart of Africa Mission,

the Unevangelized Fields Mission, the Regions Beyond Missionary Union, and a whole new breed of missions characterized in part by the faith principle but even more significantly by their yearning to go to the frontiers: they were not just "faith missions," they were "frontier missions."

It is our task today to reestablish that challenge, to take stock of our situation -- just as William Carey did in his day and Hudson Taylor did in his day, through the use of maps, charts, and statistics. If I were to choose one drawing which would capitulate the present task of world evangelization, it would be the one on the opposite page. This graphic device divides the world, first of all, into eight pieces of pie according to major cultural traditions, highlighting those three traditions which number more than 500 million people -- the Chinese, the Hindus, and the Muslims.

Next, you'll note that each piece of pie is divided into four parts indicating the degree of penetration of the Gospel. Closest to the center are two varieties of Christians; reaching out to the circumference are two varieties of non-Christians.

The crucial distinction in this chart is between those areas representing non-Christians directly evangelizable by existing churches or by presently deployed mission efforts, and those areas representing peoples who may or may not be near Christian churches but, at any rate, are culturally distant and thus reachable only by special cross-cultural evangelistic techniques, not normal back-fence evangelism. The outer periphery -- representing the second variety of non-Christians -- I have chosen to label *the Hidden Peoples*. These people are those within whose midst there is no culturally indigenous Christian church; they are the ones Paul sought especially to reach and for whose benefit his missionary career was focused.

Note that three out of four of the categories are *Unreached Peoples*, while only the fourth are *Hidden Peoples*.

The striking fact today, as in Hudson Taylor's day, is the discovery that well over 90 percent of all mission efforts are focused on the first three categories. A very small proportion of mission effort today is aimed at the Hidden Peoples. This is primarily an inadvertence. Mission efforts have been so busy and successfully and determinedly at work in the second and third categories that in many cases simple exhaustion and preoccupation account for the massive omission constituted

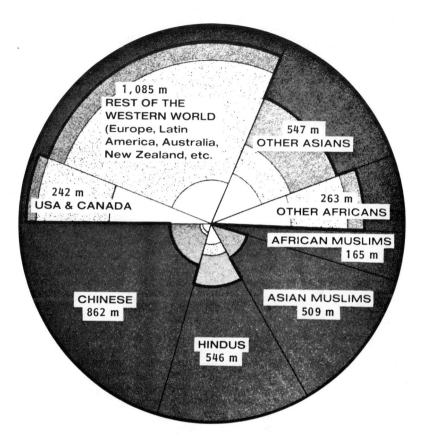

1,085 m
REST OF THE
WESTERN WORLD
(Europe, Latin
America, Australia,
New Zealand, etc.

547 m
OTHER ASIANS

242 m
USA & CANADA

263 m
OTHER AFRICANS

AFRICAN MUSLIMS
165 m

CHINESE
862 m

ASIAN MUSLIMS
509 m

HINDUS
546 m

THE WORLD IN MISSIONARY PERSPECTIVE

☐ Committed Christians

▨ Nominal Christians

▨ NonChristians within
Cultural reach

■ NonChristians Beyond the
Range of Normal Types of
Evangelism--Needing
Missionary Methods

m = 1 million

Each of the above pieces of pie is divided into 4 categories.
Each piece of pie represents a major cultural sector of the
human family. The upper 4 sectors are the *spiritual haves*
while the lower 4 are the *spiritual have nots* who have no
real chance to accept Christ.

Copyright © 1978 by Ralph D. Winter

by the mere existence of the Hidden Peoples, who number five
out of six non-Christians!

In order to look forward into the next five years seriously
and effectively, we need a checklist of the essential components of world evangelization and to set feasible targets in
the case of each one. For some years I have used a sixfold
checklist. Let us turn now to a brief survey of each point
and take note of the goals for 1984 which seem reasonably to
be related to each one.

COMPONENT ONE: MISSIOLOGY

Before he died, Dr. Charles E. Fuller made an all-out effort to found a specialized school focusing on world missions.
Dr. Donald A. McGavran, the most widely known mission strate-
gist in our time, consented to head it up. In the next ten
years, during which time I was one of the professors, that
school drew a thousand missionaries and hundreds of overseas
national church leaders, giving new visibility to formal,
systematic, disciplined, academic study of the cause of missions. That school today is still a fairly small school.
But in the cause of world evangelization it has, relatively
speaking, been very large. Dozens of missions professors and
mission executives today are the direct result of its emphasis. At the Lausanne International Congress on World Evangelization, the School of World Mission at Fuller Seminary
could claim a direct imprint on one out of ten people who attended and, outside of the Billy Graham Association itself,
had perhaps a greater influence on the rest of the participants than any other single force. Two of the plenary
speakers and several workshop leaders were from its staff.

A number of other schools have now instituted departments
of missiology -- Trinity Evangelical Divinity School and
Dallas Seminary, for example. Gordon-Conwell now has at least
one full-time missions professor. The Southwestern Baptist
Seminary at Fort Worth has big new plans, and so do a number
of other schools. All this is a necessary step in the right
direction if we are to become serious again about fulfilling
the Great Commission. No one could be happier than Dr.
McGavran, who has often observed that with at least 7,000 fur-
loughing missionaries in the U.S. at any time, there could
well be ten such Schools of World Mission, with seven full-
time professors in each of them without exaggerating the need
for missiology -- the disciplined study of the Christian mission movement.

Growing out of efforts by the School of World Mission faculty is the American Society of Missiology, the world's largest scholarly society for the study of missions, having 600 members, and producing the scholarly journal on the subject of missions, *Missiology*, which has the largest circulation in the world of any such journal.

By 1984, in the component of missiology it seems clear that certain new steps must be taken:

A. We can already see that an extremely significant impact has come from even a modest amount of disciplined evaluation and review of the mission movement. But by 1984 we need more schools of mission, more centers of missiological research. Every seminary must do its share. Each Christian college must make sure that all its students graduate with a solid grasp not just of the secular facts of our world, but also of the patterns and content of God's relentless, redemptive efforts across today's world.

B. Right now the American evangelical public is donating to mission research only one-tenth of one percent of the money given to missions. Yet mission researchers are struggling with impossible burdens of data collecting and processing. There are still at least 16,750 human sub-societies without a Christian church of any sort. By 1984 every single one of these must be encompassed by at least prayerful research and planning by missiologists in cooperation with mission agencies.

C. By 1984 the entire Yale Divinity School Day Missions Library, the best in the English-speaking world, should be available in the form of two file cabinets of microfiche cards, and it should be available in at least fifty strategic locations around the world. This is under study at the moment. It will take twenty customers at $30,000 each to put this $2 million library into that form. A research tool of this sort is of inestimable value to missiologists.

D. By 1984 evangelicals must have a greatly heightened sensitivity for the fascinating cultural differences represented by the various peoples of the world. The recent Consultation on Muslim Evangelism emphasized the impossibility of simply trying to win "Muslims" as a bloc -- Muslims who speak close to a thousand different languages and who are no more similar to each other than American Pentecostals are similar to Ethiopian Orthodox Christians. The same principle holds for the people of every religion and country of the world. We must reach them in their own languages, their own

culture, their own social classes. Missiologists must recognize as one of their primary tasks the dissemination of such
missiological insights. Like John R. Stott in his recent
article about Islam (*Christianity Today*, November, 1978), we
must speak and write so as to capture the American evangelical
public with the insights God has given so that the church will
stand behind their missionaries who try to put such principles
into practice. Missiologists have a responsible role to play
in the next five years. But theirs is only one facet of the
task that must be done.

COMPONENT TWO: IMPLEMENTATION

Coming back from Lausanne in 1974, it became increasingly
clear to me that there was something desperately lacking.
Missiology was not enough. As scholars and researchers, we
had sat in our famous "ivory towers," but someone would have
to put legs on the ideas being born. We desperately needed
an implementing organization designed to implement the birth
of other organizations.

Thus arose the William Carey Institute for Evangelism and
Church Growth. Its first organizational "baby" was the Association of Church Missions Committees. Just what its name implies, the ACMC's members are not individuals but mission
committees represented by delegates who attend the annual
ACMC conference. By 1984 this organization may well be sponsoring annually the largest meeting on the subject of missions in the United States, and by then its membership could
easily be 10,000 churches, but should be 50,000. Now, since
the time when the ACMC was implemented into existence, at
least six other organizations have gained corporate status
through the help of the William Carey Institute, and the WCI
will no doubt go on serving in this highly specialized "implementing" function.

The U.S. Center for World Mission is itself one of the
organizations helped into existence by the WCI. During the
last twenty-four months, it has gained tax-exempt status and
raised $1.5 million toward a $15 million founding budget.
Its purpose is to be a servant to all evangelical mission
agencies in locating and describing the 16,750 unpenetrated
populations of this planet and in broadening the base of mission support in the U.S. Its exclusive focus is upon the
2.5 billion "hidden" people -- those populations beyond the
outreach of any existing mission or church.

Because the task is so large, the USCWM is seeking the implementation of sixty other sister centers in key spots around
the world. One which is not totally independent but has almost identical vision is the Scottish Mission Center, founded
by WEC in Glasgow in June, 1977. We are in close cooperation
with this center. Other beginnings have been made in India,
Hong Kong, and Korea. But it is an especially delicate task
to implement the formation of an *overseas* organization. It
is no longer possible to go around the world telling people
what to do. Therefore, the approach of the USCWM has been to
answer inquiries from national leadership in other countries
and as tactfully as possible encourage parallel efforts.

By 1984, then:

A. We would hope that every major region of the world can
boast of a center of the genre which focuses on the "*least
reached*" people of the world -- the Hidden People -- giving
special emphasis to those within its own boundaries and providing Christians within those countries missiological insight
on how to reach them.

B. With IBM and now Xerox vying with AT&T for the routine
use of satellites for document transmission, we may hope to
see some exciting possibilities for effective communication
between the various points of initiative in the Christian
world mission. Both sister centers focusing on the frontier
and more generalized schools of missions must be able to exchange data rapidly, mobilizing for a cause rather than just
for the fun of research.

C. We must have a popular magazine reporting on the entire
spectrum of the cause of missions, treating what is being done
by all mission agencies around the world. It is desperately
important for there to be a rapid flow of information from one
point to another on the vast worldwide cutting edge of the
Christian world mission. There is not now a single periodical
in the English language which attempts to give this whole
picture.

D. Another equally important magazine is one which will
report on what missions are *not now doing*. This could be a
monthly picture magazine that will describe, issue by issue,
an unreached people of the Hidden variety, and describe them
from God's own perspective. It should be as graphic, popular
in style, and as high quality as the *National Geographic*, but
editorially should be openly aware of the problems and

spiritual darkness which a truly awakened evangelical conscience will perceive.

   E.   There absolutely must be, under God, a recrudescence
of the Student Volunteer Movement for Foreign Missions, and
the Laymen's Missionary Movement. People do not act individu-
ally, despite Americanistic cultural assumptions. Only if all
of us can go out of our way to nurture, sponsor, and support
a new student-led missionary movement will we surmount the
great barriers to appropriate expansion of missionary muscle
in this and other countries. The Student Volunteer Movement
for Foreign Missions, at a time when college enrollments were
one-thirty-seventh their present size, swept everything before
it, launched 20,000 people overseas with 80,000 highly committed and extensively educated mission supporters left behind
to hold the ropes. While there is nothing remotely comparable
to it today, there is nothing preventing the re-emergence of
that kind of movement if men in leadership positions today
will lend their weight to the extent that D. L. Moody did
back then.

   The Laymen's Missionary Movement, for example, virtually
unknown today, was the inevitable reverberation as the SVM
college students hit their thirties and forties and began to
take over businesses, banks, etc. In their after hours they
met for prayer and study about missions and organized themselves into the Laymen's Missionary Movement with 3,500 of-
fices across the nation. During the course of a single year,
missions banquets for its members were held in seventy-five
cities across this nation, averaging more than a thousand
businessmen per banquet. It is no wonder that within seven
years (between 1906 and 1914) mission giving in America was
quadrupled. Could it happen again? It happened then because
not only those who went as missionaries, *but also those who
stayed home had been caught up in a movement and highly educated on missions while still in college.* Those who stayed
did not forget those who went.

   We would hope that by 1984 we would have at least a 50 percent increase -- an additional $350 million per year -- for
missions. These things do not just happen. Our implementing
agencies must work and pray toward such specific ends before
God will bring it to pass.

COMPONENT THREE: RECRUITS

   Some of what we have already mentioned under *Implementation*
broaches the subject of recruits. One of the most notable

phenomena relating to this subject is the once-every-three-years Urbana Missionary Convention. This was created to carry forward the tradition of the Student Volunteer conventions and as a convention it does so admirably. The convention hall at the University of Illinois campus at Urbana simply cannot accommodate more than 18,000 people. The need for many small rooms in addition makes it difficult to find a better location. However, if the growth rate between 1973 and 1976 were projected, the meeting that could presumably be held in 1985 would have 65,000 students. (In 1976 5,000 were turned away.)

The difference between the Urbana series of meetings and those of the Student Volunteer Movement, however, is the fact that the latter was an all-year "missions only" student movement. InterVarsity has very effectively stressed generalized Christian discipleship. Both IV and Campus Crusade function in the campus world something like military chaplaincies, reaching where churches at a distance from any campus cannot easily reach. They are crucially valuable and are as broad-spectrum as are the denominations in their function. Inter-Varsity Press, serving as it does the entire spectrum of student needs and interests, has, out of something like 200 books and sixty booklets, only a handful which touch upon the subject of missions. By contrast, the SVM established a literature base which boasted over 100 documents on nothing but different aspects of the cause of missions. In the days of the SVM, Sunday School literature was saturated with lessons and allusions to missions. And the burgeoning youth ministry of the Christian Endeavor Movement built into its program a missionary emphasis every month.

But we cannot gain all our cues from the past. We must analyze on its own merits the plight of the student today who goes to Urbana and makes a serious decision to become open to God's will for service abroad. Because of IV's effective outreach on *secular* campuses, the vast majority of the Urbana students do not come from Christian colleges. Thus a few moments of inspiration and excitement at Urbana have to last many students for the remainder of their college careers. I have been involved for five years in an experiment related to this situation, and *I believe* that much more than occasional conferences are necessary. *What is required (and highly possible) is nothing less than a significant mutation in higher education.*

This will require a bit of explanation. At the Urbana Convention in 1970, 8 percent of the students signed the "available for overseas" cards. In December of 1973, the convention recorded an utterly unprecedented jump to 28 percent signing

those cards. At that point I found it easy to gain broad
backing for a specialized follow-through summer program that
would offer signers college-credit courses undergirding them
with biblical, historical, and international perspective on
the Christian world mission. A single twenty-second reference
by Leighton Ford on the Hour of Decision, for example, brought
out four additional students at the last minute that first
summer in 1974. Every summer since then and twice during the
winter a similar specialized course has been set up with the
collaboration of dozens of outstanding missions professors and
executives. Several hundred students have now obtained cred-
its which they can transfer back to the state universities and
secular colleges from which they have come. This experiment
seems to offer a prototype which with care can be greatly
expanded.

In the early years this special transferable program took
place on the Wheaton College campus. More recently it has
been held at the University of Colorado, and this past summer
on our campus in Pasadena. The campus in Pasadena is braced
for 700 students who will come in and go out every single semester or quarter, a new group three or four times a year.

The fact is that students need a special education just to
know the uncensored facts of our world today. The cause of
missions is not a simple phenomenon. Common impressions are
mainly wrong. Test yourself out! How many of you, drawing
on conventional wisdom, would find it easy to believe that
five out of six non-Christians in the world today are beyond
the normal evangelistic range of any church or mission whatsoever? The cause of the Christian mission is the most sustained, consistent effort of its size in the annals of mankind,
and absolutely nothing has ever had the degree of impact on
the nations and peoples of the world in proportion to the effort invested. Nevertheless, no student, even if he assidu-
ously follows the efforts of his own denomination overseas or
any three or five missions you can choose, would ever conclude
that 85 percent of all the schools in Africa are there because
of missions. What he knows is only a slice of the picture at
best. Who will integrate for him the fact most Christians in
India live in South India, but that Northeast India is where
you find in the total population the highest percentage of
Christians? And in what course of the state university would
he find out, even in general, how those Christians got there?
*He may be able to get a course on the history of jazz, but
very few state universities or secular colleges (or even
Christian liberal arts colleges) offer a course precisely on
the history of the Christian mission.*

But I am leading up to an even more serious proposal than our own transferable program on Christian missions. There is something basically and radically wrong with the state of affairs confronting the evangelical community in America as regards higher education. If 34 percent of Americans by George Gallup's poll consider themselves born again, then almost four million college students come from born-again homes. But even if you estimate that there are only 1.4 million dedicated evangelical students in college at any given time, you discover that 90 percent of all such students have to be in secular colleges and universities, not in Christian schools. I ask you: is it reasonable that 90 percent of our best and most dedicated young people would never darken the door of a Christian college campus? Or to state it differently, that we would give four years of exclusive Christian college environment to just 10 percent of our evangelical young people?

I talked to a pastor recently who has 600 college students in his church every Sunday during the academic year. He says that he pours his heart and soul out for the benefit of those students Sunday after Sunday, and hopes at best to get them converted to Christ and into the Word. But he can't even wave at the much larger problem they face as they trudge back to their university classrooms, face courses in philosophy, literature, history, and science that day after day raise horrendous issues with which the local church on Sunday cannot possibly cope.

Last year Leighton Ford made reference to a lawyer who felt it possible "to offer proof of the establishment of secular humanism in given public schools ... (which) directly attacks Christian values." A great deal more could be said about that. But I am almost more concerned about what the schools do *not* teach rather than what they *do* teach. Attacks and criticisms we can grapple with, but the total absence of certain kinds of data is much more subtle and difficult to handle.

For example, I have a brand new Oxford University Press book entitled, *A Concise History of the American People*. Two of the three authors are well-known, highly respected scholars, and the book will no doubt find its place in many secular, perhaps even some Christian, schools. To an American college student I feel that what God has or has not done in American history is a watershed. This is the arena of the work of the Holy Spirit in a distinctive sense for those of us who are citizens of this country. From the time of de Tocqueville to the present, thinking Europeans have mused at the difference that is America. Yet even cursory research reveals we could

have had a revolution of the French sort were it not for the
great revivals which swept our country again and again, before
and during the last century. These produced instead the basic
social reforms that form the very underpinning of our modern
sensibilities and give us the ethical fabric of our country.
As a result, no country in the history of the world has given
more to the cause of missions than the U.S. Virtually all of
the elite women's colleges in the East (Vassar, Wellesley,
Radcliffe, Smith, Mt. Holyoke, etc.) were originally founded
to train women for missions. Yet in this book there is no
reference to missions, nor to the great revivals. "Missions"
is not even in the index once. The most powerful single organization in the promotion of the Great Commission in the
entire history of man was the Student Volunteer Movement, born
in America and over 100,000 strong. It is totally absent from
this book. But not even the YMCA is mentioned here, perhaps
because as an agent of reform today it is *sleeping*, and yes-
terday it was much too *evangelistic*. But hundreds of similar
things are left out!

Thus, when I see how extens_ ̄ our secularized education
had edited out the facts of God's w_   our own immediate
past, and I reflect upon the fact that m_ ᵒf our professors
in our Christian schools come from just suc_ ₑcular university traditions, I wonder when we're going to arouse ourselves to turn back the creeping secularism that is sucking
out our very life's blood. It is affecting not only our missionary candidates coming from secular backgrounds, who, when
they come, are thereby ill-prepared and misinformed. It also
increasingly affects those from our Christian schools because
their professors have generally also come from such secular
educational backgrounds.

Fortunately, something fairly simple can actually be done
right now about this monstrous situation. In Pasadena we have
established what is perhaps the first one-semester college in
the U.S. devoted exclusively to transfer education. With 700
going in and out each semester, it can only handle 2,100 students per year! We need not be alone. Any Christian college
can set aside space for 100 students going in and coming out
each semester, transferring back to the state unviersities
and secular colleges from which they have come. A great deal
of urgent scholarly effort will be necessary, however, to give
the proper clues and cues necessary for a complete re-educa-
tion in one semester, to put back in what was consciously or
unconsciously censored out. But it can and must be done!

There is no way that evangelicalism in America has any serious future if 90 percent of its younger generation is being undermined on a wholesale basis year after year into the future. The campus organizations like Campus Crusade, Inter-Varsity, and Navigators can play an important catalytic role in massive transmigration of the sort we are talking about. Scholarly societies like the American Scientific Affiliation, Faith in History, the Evangelical Psychological Association, the Evangelical Theological Association, the American Society of Missiology, etc., must roll up their sleeves and provide the basic materials for a serious counter-education to take place. I'm not suggesting superficial or sensational "truth squads" that will barnstorm secular campuses on a hit-and-run basis, but rather serious scholarship that will supplement and complement long before it will attack.

What must we. then do by 1984?

A. By then at least 20,000 annually of the estimated one million dedicated evangelical students in secular higher education must be involved in transfer programs of the type described. But if 20,000, why not 200,000? The latter figure is possible if only one-half of all the facilities now used exclusively for a four-year Christian higher education were made available to students who otherwise really have no chance. Why should some students get four years while others get none? Massive change is necessary, not just for the sake of the missionary movement, although *that is the litmus test*. *No* serious Christian should have to be exposed to an unrelieved four years of secular, humanistic (or worse) brainwashing.

B. There must be the student movement we have already mentioned under our section entitled, *Implementation*. If there is such a movement, it must be possible on 16-foot television screens and satellite communications to have simultaneous Urbana-type conventions in five or more locations around the U.S. Also similar structures must be possible for the Christian young people in the so-called "mission lands."

C. A vast new literature is necessary. College students have very little to read on the subject of the Christian world mission compared to what the Student Volunteer Movement offered. The TEAM missions periodical designed for college students, called *Wherever*, is a superb step in the right direction.

COMPONENT FOUR: FUNDS

Where there is a will, there is a way. The necessary funds
for the cause of missions are rarely the root problem. In the
past and probably in the future, as young people head for the
field, the funds follow. But it is necessary to give attention to the subject of funding if only because, like everything else, some approaches are more effective than others.
The deterioration of vision on the subject of missions is reflected in the fall-off of effective giving. Forty years ago
most Americans were really poor. Our affluence is distinctly
a post-Second World War phenomenon. *We once gave a great deal
out of the little we had. Today we give very little out of
the great deal we have.* Despite all the moaning and groaning
about inflation, the financial problems of today's evangelicals revolve around luxuries, not necessities.

It is probable that evangelicals spend twice as much on pet
food as they do on missions. Donald Grey Barnhouse used to
say that Americans give to missions the price of a hi-fi record. That is still true. If we were all giving all we could,
how is it that some churches give twenty times as much to missions as other equally affluent congregations? In the first
years of its operation, the Association of Church Missions
Committees chewed through $50,000 in its operational budget,
but was able to measure the increase in giving as a direct result of its efforts to be $1,665,000 per year. It is as
though every dollar invested in the ACMC produced twenty-three
dollars given to missions. If you want to really multiply
your money, support the ACMC!

*The lifestyle clause in the Lausanne Covenant is being in-
creasingly discussed, but rarely in reference to the context
in which it was first penned -- that is, in relation to world
evangelization.* It is obvious that we must not discuss lifestyle as a mere ascetic ritual or even as a health trip which
will benefit ourselves more than anybody else. But we are so
glued to our possessions and our security that something truly
mighty has to happen. Try yanking a pair of sharp scissors
out of the hands of a small child. Offer the child an orange,
and the scissors are automatically discarded. Try yanking a
motorcyle out of the life of a teenage boy who lovingly dis-
mantles and reassembles it in a glowing ritual. But then a
girl appears! She is not quite so fascinated by the parts
scattered on the garage floor, though she may survive one or
two dates of that sort. It may soon be that dust will gather
on the motorcycle, assembled or unassembled, as *expulsive*

power of a new affection rearranges priorities, and some things grow strangely dim in the light of others.

The "expulsive power of a new affection" was the phrase wielded by John Wesley to describe what was happening in the early days of the Evangelical Awakening in England. The rigor of many years of simple life and self-imposed austerities in his past was now suddenly made purposeful as the evangelical experience at Aldersgate replaced the legalism of the Holy Club at Oxford. But the exuberance and momentum of the Evangelical Awakening did not result in a John Wesley driving around in a Cadillac. When he died, his possessions could be lifted by one hand.

A few weeks ago *Time* magazine -- give them credit -- jerked us all up with an all-out story on the abandoned children of Brazil, so seriously divorced from proper food, clothing, and family affection that experts say fourteen million of them can never become normal adults. The problem is not a lack of wealth in Brazil, but a lack of love. And yet to reach out with an evangelical message that can elicit that love in Brazil takes funds -- cold, hard cash. The cause of the world's children and their need for love certainly merits sacrifice on our part. How, under heaven, can we live out our days in affluent isolation from these real problems both at home and abroad? How, under heaven, can we choose the welfare of a house cat over that of a Brazilian child?

There is no agency nor any combination of agencies on the face of the earth that can reach into Brazil and dole out the proper food, clothing, and affection that these children need. Yet, in actual fact, all of those resources are within the situation itself if only the hearts of the fathers in Brazil can be turned to the children in the way it happened when George Whitefield stormed the Atlantic seaboard in the eighteenth century in the Great Awakening of the Middle Colonies, when, for the first time, pictures of children began to appear on the mantles and dressers of American homes. There is no technological answer. But Christ has an answer! And it takes money!

In my opinion, the most trenchant proposal for massive but practical change in the use of money in the hands of evangelicals is for the mission agencies of America to allow and encourage lay supporters voluntarily to adopt the same level of support accorded their missionaries on furlough. Parkinson's Law says that "expenses always rise to meet income." But it seems to me there is another law that could be enunciated:

"where available income falls, or is voluntarily decreased, expenses inevitably and naturally fall."

Picture a man and wife, committed evangelicals, looking anxiously at each other, standing in front of the fireplace in a home in an affluent suburb. Their eighteen-year-old daughter, the hospital reports, has cancer. It will cost them $18,000 to deal with the situation. Can they handle it? Will they think twice about the expense? How about all those other daughters around the world whom God equally loves?

We must ask God to lay on our hearts the real people of the real world. The best way a family can do that, I am convinced, is to affiliate itself with a mission agency that will treat it as a missionary family, but allow it to support itself, in effect, by channelling its normal income through the mission's financial office, the rest of its income stored up, being available to the family but saved up for the use of evangelism around the world. Most evangelical families will indeed have a surplus left over if they do that, which to properly use they will then have to pray new kinds of prayers and learn new kinds of things. By this method, assuming the average evangelical family will turn up at least $2,000 per year (beyond the support level defined by the mission agency to which they are affiliated), 100,000 families could free up $200 million per year for the cause of the Gospel.

Thus, by 1984 there are certain goals we must surely aim for:

A. I believe it is reasonable to suggest that by then, 100,000 evangelical family units (that's only one out of 160 of the estimated number in the U.S.) could become identified and economically associated with some specific mission agency. The resulting giving to missions would raise the total mission giving in America to an annual $1 billion dollars! If the new total sounds like a lot of money, it is far, far less than evangelicals right now pay for coffee!

B. Of this additional amount, I would devoutly hope that at least 25 percent will be designated specifically for new work among Hidden Peoples -- the five out of six non-Christians who are beyond the normal evangelistic outreach of any existing church or mission.

C. Indeed, by 1984 we could hope that at least 5,000 evangelical congregations would clearly distinguish between their "regular missions" and their "frontier missions" budgets.

COMPONENT FIVE: THE MISSION AGENCIES

We come now to our fifth category. Seven hundred mission agencies fueled by $700 million a year is the rough picture for North America. This vast mechanism of human organizations represents almost two centuries of dedicated, prayerful development. Agencies which have been started more recently have profited both by the pattern of the past and the present favorable disposition of society, so that even the newer agencies are in effect part of a lengthy development in United States history.

It is curious that when most people think about missions, they think about mission agencies. They are immediately aware of the *structures* which collect money and people and send teams to foreign countries. At the same time, some of our people often reflect on the vast world yet to win and *forget all about these agencies in panicky thinking* which leads to all kinds of other alternatives. In fact, I see five alternatives to conventional mission structures, all of which have their merits but none of which can really do the job without the traditional approach.

The Renewers

One alternative results from the success of some pastors in the United States in leading their churches to new life through a special type of renewal, small-group fellowship, charismatic experience, or discipleship program. These pastors sometimes conclude that missions can continue only if all churches everywhere, here and abroad, have that same experience. Thus they feel it doesn't do any good to send more missionaries unless the missionaries go out with the distinctive insights of a particular new renewal movement in the U.S. Their concerns are thus focused upon improving churches, whether they be U.S. churches or foreign churches. This is, of course, all to the good, but it will not in and of itself make sure that people who have never heard will soon hear. It is an insidious fact that all too often as we devote ourselves to the renewal of ourselves or our nation, we find, like Napoleon going into Russia, that we never achieve our ultimate objective.

The Exposers

A second approach is examplified by the vast new development in the last twenty years of short-term work. Operation Mobilization people and Youth With a Mission have probably

sent 100,000 young people out in short-term evangelizing work
over the last twenty years. And if you add the short-term
programs spawned in parallel by the traditional missions, we
behold a veritable avalanche of young people who have gone
overseas for at least a short period.

It must be suggested, however, that good as short-term service is, a short period does not allow systematic, thorough
language study nor the building up of long-term confidences
with the people to whom they go, both of which are really essential in order for the work of Christ to be deeply rooted
in a strange country. But just as the Second World War hurled
millions of young Americans out across the world and they came
back with their eyes full of needs, challenges, and opportunities, setting up a hundred new mission agencies, so these
"exposure" organizations today are doing a tremendous amount
of good in confronting other young people with the unreached
peoples of the world.

The Specializers and Emphasizers

Many of the new organizations which came into existence
after the Second World War were service agencies, serving
existing mission agencies by emphasizing and assisting with
some one aspect of existing work. This might be medical as-
sistance, relief, literature, or radio evangelism. Specialized agencies are needed in all such areas. Wycliffe Bible
Translators, for example, is essentially a service mission
providing the service of Bible translation and depending heavily on the continuation of existing missions to reach out and
to enfold the converts which result. This vast plethora of
specialized agencies is an absolute Godsend, but it is true
that such agencies alone cannot do the job. Child Evangelism
Fellowship, for example, specializes in winning children to
Christ and then through those children tries to reach whole
families and bring them into the church. What church? Who
will start churches?

Thus, we see that the specializers and emphasizers in the
long run have to depend on the existence of churches already
planted by normal church-planting mission organizations if
their work is to succeed.

The Self-Supporters

A fourth type of alternative approach is gaining a great
deal of ground and needs to be emphasized even more than it
is. We may call it the approach of the so-called "non-profes-

sional missionary," one who is essentially a layman working overseas for some foreign country or an American company and who, thus, has his way paid right into the foreign situation where the Gospel needs to be preached. Business-related Americans overseas today outnumber missionaries by 100 to 1, and it is folly if we fail to exploit more effectively this vast paid-for reservoir of talent. A fairly high percentage of these are devout Christians, and with a little bit of additional guidance and coordination, they could do far more than they are doing for the cause of the Great Commission. They are able not only to witness to the national leaders within the range of their activity, but they can also reach other Americans who are just as lost as any of the citizens of the countries in which they work.

Such people are not likely, however, to reach rural, village, or common people since they are not within the range of their normal association. And insofar as their days are jammed with high pressures and responsibilities, they are not much more likely to succeed in a cross-cultural missionary task by living overseas than is a busy layman in this country likely to be able to go out and plant in his own city a church composed of people who speak some other language. *The important thing to understand about this very worthwhile category is that it is not the same as the tent-making work which Paul did.* Paul's was a still more specialized form of nonprofessional work. First of all, Paul did not go primarily because of the job he had. His secular work was a stopgap, employed only part of the time. Second, he was the absolute owner of his business, an entrepreneur. He was not subject to someone else's office hours nor to the requirements of an organization in which he had no control. Third, his was a special kind of *portable* job; he could readily move from one place to another as the work of the Gospel required. Nonprofessional Christians overseas, then, are not the wave of the future; they are *an* important wave of the *present*. Further utilization of their efforts is important, but this category is not a panacea for world evangelization.

"Let the Overseas Churches (and Missions?) Do the Job" Syndrome

A fifth alternative to traditional missions is the assumption that national church leadership overseas can and should pick up the slack of the remaining job. The so-called "third world missions" constitute a newly observed phenomenon which has been in existence for at least a hundred years or more in many parts of the globe and is surely a very vital and

important thing to see flourish. In my estimation, the
greatest single mistake in the past of the foreign mission
movement was that there was no clearly developed planning
whereby not only national *churches* were created overseas, but
national mission agency structures were developed as well.
This did happen in the celebrated case of the Evangelical Missionary Society of West Africa, which is associated with ECWA
(the Evangelical Church of West Africa), the church established by the Sudan Interior Mission. It has 300 people doing
home missions and in some cases cross-cultural missions in
Nigeria and nearby countries, for the most part. The Christian and Missionary Alliance, more than any other mission I
know, has made sure its mission field churches get involved
in missionary endeavors (not just evangelism among their own
people). Another celebrated example, for which no mission
agency can take credit, is the Friends Missionary Prayer Band
of South India, which has 150 missionaries working cross-
culturally, learning the foreign languages of northern India.
May this sort of thing increase!

However, it is probably true that almost all the agencies
which are promoting the sending of funds directly overseas to
"national missionaries" are sending such funds to people who
will not really do *missionary* work as such, so much as reach
out to their *own people* in normal evangelism. That is to say,
they do a type of local evangelism within the culture where
the church is already established. Yet, as we have already
noted earlier, five out of six non-Christians do not live
within the normal evangelistic range of any overseas church.
Virtually all such "national missionaries" are more exactly
categorized as "local evangelists," many of whom really ought
to be supported by their own people. The tragedy is that most
people in this country assume that all work overseas is "missions," and they do not make the distinction between local
evangelists using their own language to win their own people
(evangelism) and those rare nationals and expatriates who are
penetrating cultures where there is no church at all (missions). The latter task is just as difficult for a person
from South India going to northern India as it is for a Korean
going to North India or for an American going to North India.

But one difference is the fact that the American going to
North India comes from a homeland with almost 200 years of
disciplined background and experience in the tradition of language learning, anthropological studies, and effective mission
support structures. Sad to say, most overseas-born missions
are still in their infancy. The third-world missions of Asia
and Africa are certainly one of the most important single

elements in the picture, and we must do all we can possibly do to aid them without harming them. But we are grossly mistaken if we think we can, at this point, simply wash our hands of further mission work and let these overseas agencies do the rest of the job. *Thus, we must count as the most dangerous heresy in missions today the simplistic statement that the national can do the job.* For most nonbelievers, as we have seen, there is no national Christian in the picture at all. There is no church in that culture. Thus, a Christian of any sort has to be an outsider, whether he is from the same country or from another. Furthermore, local prejudice barriers between two subcultures are often so high that nearby Christians of another tribe or culture may actually face far greater prejudices than would someone coming from another country entirely. In any case, this type of evangelism for both the Christians within that country and for us is a truly missionary task, not an easy bit of near-neighbor evangelism.

There is simply no substitute for the obligation for Christians everywhere to do what they can to send people to the 16,750 cultures which are not yet penetrated by the Gospel. This is so big a task it would be foolhardy for Americans to feel it is no longer their job. The mission agencies in America today are human organizations. Their leadership grows old; younger leadership comes in; they have their ups and downs. But those agencies, their discipline, their dedication, their devotion, their supporters, their prayer structure, and their fine root structure reaching out into America represent the very cream of devotion and spiritual resources in America today. We must not doubt this. We must not overlook this resource and bypass it in any way.

On the other hand, severe stresses are to be found in the present picture. Galloping inflation both in this country and far worse in most mission lands has had the actual effect of substantially reducing the impact of American giving to missions in the last four years, despite the literal increase of giving in terms of the number of dollars. This is especially true in light of the shrinking value of the dollar. In fact, the dollar balance of payments is so serious a problem for Americans today that we must face the possibility that within the time span between now and 1984 it will become literally impossible to send money out of this country. It may well be that the U.S. government will freeze the ceiling for mission agencies at existing rates of outflow, and then later on ask for a 10, 20, or 50 percent reduction down to zero. This will mean that self-supporting missions of all kinds with all their deficiencies will become more and more urgent and important, and all mission agencies must take this into account.

Holding in mind the distinction between Paul's work and the average overseas Christian professional in secular work, it is perfectly possible for agencies to begin to concentrate on the type of tent-making Paul did. For example, the teaching of English as a second language (TESL) is a skill in demand in every city of the world, even in the United States. The person who is skilled in this way can support himself, not only in the so-called *open* countries, but even in the *closed* countries. I would not doubt that within ten years it will be possible for 50,000 Americans to find employment teaching English in the People's Republic of China, if they really know what they are doing. Note that it is not good enough just to be able to speak English. This is why in Pasadena we have a specialized program in teaching TESL. It is a first-rate tent-making skill. Another tent-making skill is in the area of other kinds of education. There are at least a thousand jobs open in Africa today which used to be funded by missions but now are backed by low but adequate local government salaries. The same thing is true for nurses, but especially nurses with the new practitioner training. This is why in Pasadena we have established a nurse practitioner program. Yes, the dollar crunch will make all this sort of missions more urgent than ever.

Looking toward 1984, I feel there are a number of things mission agencies must pray for and work toward:

A. I would look for the "Renewers" to become conscious of the essential worldwide mission outworking of their efforts. I believe that no Christian family or church anywhere in the world can be completely healthy if it is not daily praying and working toward the reaching of those who sit in darkness beyond the outreach of any existing church or mission. *Renewal cannot precede outreach if outreach is a condition of renewal.*

B. I would hope that the traditional missions would be much more closely and happily related to the "Exposure" mechanisms, both their own short-term programs and those of other groups. Let's see much more of the fabulous collusion between eight standard missions and Language Institutes for Evangelism (LIFE), that superb church-planting, short-term program working in Japan. Also, hopefully, almost every major mission will have carefully investigated the concept of a youth division by 1984.

C. I would hope that the many relatively recent "Emphasizer" missions would be able to see themselves as normal, desirable, specialized service agencies, serving the larger Christian cause in which the church-planting agencies are more likely foundational. This would work out in part as such new organizations show up and participate (as, for example, the Agape Movement of Campus Crusade now does) at the annual EFMA or IFMA Executive Retreats.

D. A great deal of implementation is necessary among the vast numbers of potentially effective self-supporting believers working in mission lands. Every major city in the non-Western world needs at least one full-time person helping these self-supported evangelicals already there to be equipped and effective in a cutting-edge spiritual ministry among those with whom they alone are in contact. But we also need massive tooling up for true tent-making missions of the kind we have defined. Christian colleges need special programs, especially on the graduate level, in small-capital entrepreneur-type activities suited to this type of ministry. Mission agencies must urgently move in this direction. Why not 5,000 of the true tent-making type of missionaries by 1984?

E. There must be an international directory of cross-cultural, frontier mission agencies. Hopefully, the Missions Commission of the World Evangelical Fellowship will contribute to this. So also the Asia Missions Association, and the many new country-level associations of missions. The long-proposed World Consultation of Frontier Missions in 1980 will hopefully raise the visibility of this type of organization. Only as the real thing becomes visible and prominent will the other things now being confused for frontier missions be distinguished for the good but different things they are.

COMPONENT SIX: SYNTHESIS

We now come to the final and most important dimension of the necessary push forward to do everything within our power to complete the Great Commission for our generation by 1984.

I speak of the need for bringing the Great Commission back into the center of attention of the Christian movement. I'm calling this *synthesis*. It has been a long time since the Great Commission was central to the evangelical movement in America. But just because it has almost always been a marginal matter, except for a brief period during the peak of the Student Volunteer Movement, this does not mean God *intends* it to be marginal. Last year the number of lines on a page

concerned with missions in the printed volume of the Consultation on Future Evangelical Concerns could almost be counted
on the fingers of one hand. This year it would be very easy
as we look into the future to have, as the disciples did, a
different agenda from that of our Lord. Remember, they seemed
to be just as interested in the future as He was.

But what specifically can we look for as a synthesis of
God's will for the evangelical movement?

I want to say frankly that I believe the Billy Graham Association and Billy Graham personally constitutes the most
likely human impetus in our world today for the achievement
of the synthesis of which I speak. There is no question that
in America today missions is at the margin. There must be a
way forward so that world evangelization can become central to
the evangelical movement. This is not an option. The whole
of the Bible underscores the cosmic paradox that if we seek
our own survival, we will lose it. If we do not make central
a new dynamic for the survival of the world's people -- the
little people God loves in the shadows of our own nation and
in the dark corners of the earth -- we have no reason to leave
this room. There is no other viable mission to which we
may return.

Synthesis takes place, in my definition here, when the
whole Christian community centers its attention together on
the highest priorities -- which do not happen to include the
survival of our nation or even of our evangelical movement.
That is precisely *secondary*, if I read the Bible correctly.
Billy Graham has brought together the committed Christian
movement more than any other person in our time. He has done
this by means of crusades, and he has dealt with leadership
in Congresses, which he has sponsored indirectly. At the risk
of seeming presumptuous, I am profoundly convinced that there
needs to be more than crusades here and there from time to
time. Just as the nation of Israel in the Bible had its annual feast days, especially its annual Pentecost, I believe
every major region of the world must exert the effort to develop annual evangelical festivals that will synthesize the
forces of the Gospel and bring them together as if to a county
fair for a week during which a vast number of exhibits will
acquaint believers in that region with what is going on. Dozens of workshops will instruct and equip people in many ministries, and nightly meetings of a crusade variety will galva-
nize their attention to the glory of God on the recognition of
achievement and the subjection to the unfinished tasks of the
future. In all of this I would think evangelism and mission

outreach to the ends of the earth could be and must be central. Synthesizing without that evangelical centrality will not save us nor anyone else.

By 1984, then:

A. I believe we ought to have at least five major regional *annual* festivals of this kind in the United States.

B. I believe we ought to pray and hope for at least ten regions across the non-Western world to be united in prayer and festival-type annual celebrations stressing worship and recognition of the full meaning of the Divine Mandate.

C. But most of all, I pray that by then we'll have stood our ground in the face of the winds of change and uncertainty and that, as a movement, we will have escaped the present virtual imprisonment of evangelical forces in America behind the bars of the cares and riches and pleasures of this life. I simply pray that having received much, we will be willing for much to be required of us, and that we will have listened to the Lord of history and slowly replied, *"'Not my will, but thine be done'* ... *not our human agendas, but yours, O God."*

The Future of the Church:
The Essential Components of
World Evangelization

Response: J. Robertson McQuilkin

As many of us have come to expect from Ralph Winter, we have before us innovative proposals enough to occupy the entire church for the foreseeable future! Because of my conviction that he is one of the most creative thinkers in the field of missiology, I was delighted at the prospect when I was asked to respond to his presentation. Although I guessed some of the emphases in advance, I was prepared to hear some bold, new, unorthodox ideas. I have not been disappointed.

In response, then, I would like to spotlight several of his key proposals, suggest a caution concerning one of them, and indicate what I consider a major omission.

With increasing clarity and vigor Dr. Winter has held before the church the two and one-half billion "hidden people," the one out of every two persons on earth who does not even have a near neighbor to bring him the good tidings of life in Christ. Someone will have to cross cultural, language, and geographic barriers to reach these people. Since his startling and compelling presentation at Lausanne, the vision of these peoples has haunted me with increasing intensity. I pray that this vision may come into focus for all of God's people, because, without controversy, this is the great burden on the heart of God Himself.

It is distressing for me to contemplate that less than 5 percent of American Christian workers are engaged in cross-cultural ministries. Of this small missionary force only 25 percent is engaged in cross-cultural evangelism. That means one percent of our American Christian workforce is involved in *other-culture* evangelism.

As if this were not failure enough for our generation, Ralph Winter has pointed out that only a fraction of this one-percent remnant of Christian workers is deployed in *unevangelized areas.* Surely this need looms far above all other needs as the responsibility of the church in whatever future God may grant us. If we do not take this seriously and put it at the top of our agenda, whatever other good things we may do, I do not believe we will ever earn the accolade, "good and faithful servant."

Dr. Winter has suggested a number of methods for changing this picture. Let me note two of these:

First, concerning *finances*, he says that much greater financial support will be needed if we are to make headway. He suggests that large funds will be available only if we in the Western world become committed to a simple lifestyle. I have been told on good authority that Dr. Winter practices what he preaches. I know of no way to reinforce this biblical call, reiterated in the Lausanne Covenant, than for us to make a personal commitment to it.

Winter argues further that, in the light of the uncertain future of the dollar, we may be forced to send *tent-making missionaries.* He wisely defines "tent making" missionaries as those who spend a minimum of time in life support and the bulk of time in church-starting evangelism. If I sense the mood of contemporary young people at all, it seems to me that this approach should have high appeal. However, I believe we will need to identify the *kind* of employment on which a committed family can live by working only twenty hours a week. Dr. Winter suggested one or two kinds.

I recommend that the U. S. Center for World Mission takes as a major project the identifying of several such vocations for each target area of the world. This research would no doubt include experimentation and wide dissemination of the conclusions. *I also recommend* that the William Carey Institute establish a branch called Tent Makers, Inc., which will attract evangelical business people who are willing to take the risk of organizing, and, if need be, financing and training people for this type of employment. If such implementation does not take place, I do not foresee large numbers of young people moving in this direction.

More important than finance, Dr. Winter has correctly identified *people* as essential to accomplishing this task. He
suggests that a student movement comparable to the Student
Volunteer Movement is needed. He implies that one big meeting every three years will not recruit the numbers that are
needed: that a grassroots, dynamic, nationwide, and church-
wide movement is needed.

We have learned something from the history of the Student
Foreign Missions Fellowship, which was born of the deep desire
to provide that very alternative to a theologically emascu-
lated and increasingly impotent Student Volunteer Movement.
The Student Foreign Missions Fellowship moved rapidly across
Christian college and Bible college campuses. Then, in an
effort to reach Christian students on secular campuses, it
was absorbed into the InterVarsity Christian Fellowship. The
move appeared wise at the time, but SFMF has never become the
dynamic movement of the original vision. In the sixties, student leader Paul Bowers sensed this and worked toward a renewal within SFMF. I believe one reason this vision has not
been fulfilled is indicated by Ralph Winter. An independent,
missions-only movement is necessary.

I believe one other thing is necessary. The Student Volunteer Movement was characterized by *adult leadership of
church-wide eminence*. Where today are the John Motts and the
Robert Spears in evangelical leadership? We have men of great
influence in education, in evangelism, in television outreach,
in pulpiteering. But where are the giants serving the cause
of missions in the United States? I think they are not here
at this meeting because they don't exist. And that speaks
clearly of our self-chosen priorities.

As part of the solution, Dr. Winter suggests a semester
"stop out" in Christian colleges across the country. I will
need to see this succeed before I can be convinced that so
short a training period can make the radical kind of change
which Winter foresees. I think a semester in a Christian college would be a good thing, but the most I could realistically
hope for is inspiration and challenge to consider seriously
the demands of the Great Commission and the possibility of
graduate training in Bible and missions. If the U.S. Center
for World Mission or other schools which follow this model
concentrate on philosophical theology and naturalistically-
based anthropology, we will not see a flood of recruits moving out into the field. If, as Donald McGavran says, we do
not have practical, down-to-earth church-growth anthropology,
the budding idealists who have stopped out for three months

will be crushed beneath the load of premature information concerning the stupidities of past generations of missionaries
and the enormity of the task of cross-cultural communications.
They may be opened up to a wider view of God's world, may become so-called "World Christians," but not many will ever get
involved in actual other-culture church-starting evangelism.
These months would be great for recruiting but wholly inadequate for training, which Dr. Winter realizes. But recruiting
can best be done by exposure to the need, the exciting potential, and the basic teaching of the Bible on missions. The
heavy theology and anthropology must be integrated in the
later, more extensive time of actual training.

There is one approach to this problem which I believe Dr.
Winter has assumed, but which needs to be clearly and force-
fully articulated and the implications need to be thought
through and widely disseminated. God's *key* for the impossible
task which faces us is not completed, and it is not glamorous.
He gave the key when He gave Peter the keys. The *church* is
God's key to the evangelization of the world. Evangelism is
not full evangelism until proclamation becomes persuasion and
persuasion becomes parish.

We can learn from the explosive birthrate of the twentieth
century. It comes from very simple beginnings. A family of
two reproduces more than two. God's answer is his family,
local congregations. Simple. Uncomplicated. Not glamorous.
But explosive in its potential. The spiritual birthrate can
well outstrip the biological birthrate if we are prepared to
start new church "families." Few churches in the United
States are growing in newborns. One reason is plain. Church-
growth analysts for the United States return the same hard
data that overseas church-growth people have been reporting
for years: a growing church is a church in which new congregations are being established. What is wrong? Why are we
not doing it?

Ron Fisher in the current issue of *The Evangelical Missions
Quarterly* says it well:

> [Concerning] the problem of planting local churches.
> Missionaries see the need of this ministry, but most of
> them are not seeing the results they would like to.
> Why aren't they more effective? What is the root prob-
> lem? [They have not experienced nor even seen a church
> being born.]

Nor have missionaries really been trained for church-
planting. The second reason for their ineffectiveness
is conventional Christian training in North America.
Generally speaking, schools were founded to provide
for the needs of American Christianity. Only gradu-
ally did they evolve a missionary emphasis. Even
this was much influenced by the way things are done
in America.

This is especially true of seminaries ... seminary-
trained men generally are prepared to minister to an
already established "clientele": they expect to pastor
a church or teach in a school.

Seminary grads therefore may find it very difficult to
adjust to the mission field. They arrive to find very
few to ... pastor, because the task of pioneer church-
planting hasn't been accomplished. They tend to look
for a teaching position, or to get involved in a specialized ministry like student work.

It's the most natural thing in the world for them to
want to do what they're prepared to do and what makes
them feel most "at home." They may still be "in church-
planting," but it will be oriented around what they are
used to doing.

Those having difficulty coping with the situation may,
on the other hand, feel led to pioneer a new parachurch
institution or movement. They are more prepared for
this; to adjust their ministry to church-planting demands time and struggle. The more thorough the training, and the more professional it is, the greater is
the difficulty to adjust.

In the training programs of seminaries and Bible colleges
across America there is little instruction in the apostolic
gift which Paul places at the head of his list. If there is
little instruction, there are even fewer models and almost no
experience for the person who is being called of God. We need
to rethink our definition of "success." If the heroes are not
those engaged in the tough task of establishing a new congregation, young people will follow other models. We need models. And we must provide training. We have become committed
at Columbia Graduate School of Bible and Missions and Columbia
Bible College to provide the models and the training. As seminaries and Bible colleges across the land determine to do
this, we will be able to produce those who can go overseas and

get the job done. We will be identifying gifted men and
training them in a context of flexibility to adapt the form
of the church to succeed in radically different cultural
contexts.

If we take this seriously, some of our best overseas
church-starters will be brought home for extended furloughs
to train the next generation in this most important task.

We will also need to redefine "missionary." The definition
has been blurred so that the term no longer refers to one with
the gift and calling of starting churches in non-churched
areas. It now refers to anyone who serves full-time in a
church-related vocation in a culture other than his own while
being paid by Christian people from his own culture. This
leads to great confusion in recruiting and training. As a
result, we are not producing the one kind of person who is
designed by God to complete the Great Commission.

When we are prepared to radically realign our financial
priorities, give birth to a movement that will catch up tens
of thousands of our youth in a life-transforming vision of a
lost world, and train thousands of specialists in church-
starting evangelism, the church will be nearer -- and not
increasingly farther from -- the day when it can cry, *"It is
finished. The task which Thou gavest us to do, we have
accomplished."*

PART III

Scenarios

Scenario: Study Group #1

William C. Brownson, Jr.

Stimulated, stretched, and deeply stirred by the experience of these days together, we offer here our shared vision of a time to come for the church in God's world.

We see reason to expect, with Willis Harman, a heightened awareness of the extrasensory, supra-rational dimensions of human life. And, with Peter Henriot, we find nothing on the horizon to halt such trends as the proliferation of nuclear weapons, a runaway world economy, and mounting strains upon the environment.

For us, ominous evidence points toward the continued erosion of democracy, a further withering of family life, and multiplied miseries for the poor and deprived of the earth. We are in a time of troubles, and the possibilities of unprecedented catastrophe are pressingly real.

At the same time, we affirm that God has made the crucified, risen Jesus both Lord and Christ. All authority in heaven and earth belongs to Him. He rules as history's sovereign, taking the book of destiny and opening, one by one, its seals. All future events of judgment and grace are in His hands. He is building His church, and the gates of hell shall not prevail against it! We expect, by faith in His name, a church made strong and a world increasingly confronted by His claims, until He comes.

Our vision of mission comes from the triune God and His self-revealing. He so loved the world that He gave His Son.

He, the missionary God, sends us to make disciples of all the
nations. He, the mighty one who sides with the needy and the
downtrodden, calls us to be compassionate neighbors, to seek
justice, and to remember the poor. He who loves community,
who ordained the family and wants to see it together, sends
us to bind up its wounds.

We embrace God's mission, His *whole* mission. We're tired
of "wrongly dividing" His design. We want to rightly put it
together! God's one Holy Spirit has anointed us to build up
the body in love *and* to relieve the oppressed and afflicted
and to preach the reconciling Gospel to every creature. We
take to our hearts all of God's saving purpose and all who
labor to serve it.

Our initial strategy is: "all things by prayer." Our hope
for world stability lies in the God who calls us to offer sup-
plications "for all men, for kings and all in high positions
that we may lead a quiet and peaceable life," to further His
plan who "desires all men to be saved and to come to the knowledge of the truth." Our hope for church renewal lies in believing prayer to the One who opens the eyes of our hearts,
strengthens us in the inner man, roots and grounds us in caring, overwhelms us with Christ's love, and fills us with all
the fullness of God. Our hope for a vast army of Christian
workers is in Him who looks on the multitudes with compassion
and says, "The harvest is great, the laborers are few. Pray
the Lord of the harvest that He may thrust laborers into His
harvest ..." The possibility of earth-shaking transformations, undreamed-of triumphs of the Gospel in a hostile
world, burns in those prayers of the saints that are mingled
with the fire of God and cast on the earth.

Our broad strategy is a united evangelical front worldwide.
As we renounce the dead end of merely organizational mergers,
we relinquish also the hollow claim of a oneness which no one
ever sees. We want to explore every possible means to "keep
the unity of the Spirit" and to make it visible.

Our base is a church constantly reformed in values,
thought, and life, by the Spirit through the written Word;
a community of praise and proclamation; a church structured
to function as the body of Christ, to nurture family leaders
in their task and be a family to all the orphaned hearts
that cry out for one.

For creative new ways to carry out the mission, we call for
a continuing conclave of evangelical strategizers, praying

men and women with "understanding of the times" to show what God's people ought to do, and for a new network of communication alerting us regularly to the needs, perils, and opportunities of the world mission.

Can it happen in a church so wedded to the spirit of the age, so tied to questionable power structures, so tinged with Pharisaism? Only in the way of repentance, in a ruthless reappraisal of what and how we communicate, in a radical readiness to listen to prophetic voices that disturb us. "For this is the man to whom I will look, says the Lord, he that is humble and contrite in spirit and trembles at my word." Once to a chastened, broken-hearted people, mourning their children, returning to God, came a word of strong encouragement: "Keep your voice from weeping and your eyes from tears, for your work shall be rewarded, says the Lord, and they shall come back from the land of the enemy. There is hope for your future." Amen.

Scenario: Study Group #2

Richard F. Lovelace

I. HOW WILL THE 1980'S BE DIFFERENT?

A. Needs in the World

We agree with Willis Harman that America (and perhaps the
Western world and other sectors of world society) will continue to move in the post-secular trend which has been growing since the 1960's, reacting against the failures of technological materialism and seeking more and more for "religious" answers and foundations. Increasingly rapid change in
every part of the world will shatter many idolatrous systems
and produce futures shock, and these effects could also reinforce a new openness and sense of spiritual need. On the
other hand, if the 1980's bring us *either* a set of easy technological solutions to the crisis of crises, or else a con-
stellation of major disasters, the returning sense of religious need is likely to be numbed again.

During the 1980's, Christian response to *social* needs
throughout the world will either dampen or reinforce the
world's sense of *spiritual* need. "The cares of this world
and the delight in riches" are still the two main impedi-
ments to the search for the Kingdom of God. If the poor
(that is, the majority) among the world's people are oppressed by hunger and injustice, and if they observe rich
Christians either ignoring or unwittingly assisting this oppression, they will be distracted from the Gospel witness
and repelled by those who bear it.

B.   Threats to World Society and to the Church

This planet is now publicly regarded increasingly not as
a manageable spaceship, but as a terminally ill patient on
the "Critical List" and in "Intensive Care." If merely human forces and logical probabilities are all we consider,
they point toward eventual major disaster in one or more of
these forms: unlimited thermonuclear war; a collapse of
Western society into the totalitarian nightmare Orwell fore-
saw, triggered by acts of terrorism or by other precipitat-
ing factors acting upon our instability; or economic collapse.
If, as Herman Kahn hopes, we muddle through the 1980's toward
a continued and now worldwide growth of affluent, sensate humanist culture, this is still a deadly threat to the Christian
movement.

Meanwhile, new forms of paganism are rising to fill the
religious vacuum. The self-fulfillment movement is collaps-
ing the fabric of our commitment to one another and to society. Its gravitational field is warping both the liberal
sector of the church (in "liberation" movements which over-
shoot their boundaries into autonomous humanism) and "conservative" Christianity (in self-centered pietism or self-
help religion). Scientists are returning to their origins
in magic, playing with soft-core occult technology and mis-
taking this for religion, while genuine counterfeit religions, like the Unification Church and the Jones cult, ensnare
the elect as angels of light, or frighten the world as angels
of darkness. Almost all religion is afflicted with an anti-
systematic existentialism and a reliance on subjective experience unguarded by objective norms. The majority of American
society which is still irreligious is threatened by forces
which dissolve the family and foster corruption and violence.
The entertainment media in this country are still mainly in
the hands of humanists promoting anti-Christian values, or
unprincipled business interests willing to serve up whatever
sells the most. Alternate Christian media appearing now are,
so far, in danger of boring the world to death while they di-
vert the resources needed for the serious business of the
Kingdom. Critical attacks upon these and other weaknesses
among evangelicals may intensify in other parts of the church
and the humanist community, and even if these faults are corrected, the growth and the prophetic edge of a healthy evangelicalism will inevitably evoke a degree of reaction and
persecution.

The total pattern of these interrelated dangers can be used
by agents of darkness and secular prophets of despair to

intimidate the church and paralyze its initiative for world
evangelism and social healing. We consider the distractions
and introversions involved in this loss of nerve within the
church as a threat to humanity which is as serious as the
dangers themselves.

C. Opportunities *for* the Church

On the other hand, these impending dangers could function
as the greatest alarm clock in history to awaken a sleeping
church and a dying world. Those whose bed is under the Sword
of Damocles do not sleep easily. The very urgency of the
situation could drive Christians to make the sacrifices necessary to mobilize our resources for the greatest missionary
outreach within the global village which history has yet seen.
It could goad us to recognize and cross cultural boundaries
which until now we have hardly recognized. It could force
divided Christians into a level of communication and practical unity in mission strategy which could unite and reinvigorate every genuine part of the body of Christ. It could
result in our learning from our critics and being purified
instead of embittered by our persecutors.

D. Challenges *to* the Church

Neither the whole church nor the evangelical sector can
afford to wait until our faults are corrected and our ill-
nesses are healed before we move throughout the world in
concert with our brothers and sisters to advance the Kingdom
of Christ into the unreached subcultures of the world. We
must repent, reform, and reunite while we are already on the
move in redemptive proclamation and social demonstration of
the Gospel.

On the other hand, we will inevitably fail in missionary
outreach unless we are at the same time advancing in repentance and spiritual renewal. We cannot realize Isaiah's
goals without Isaiah's vision of the holy God, our personal
sin, and the sins of the structures and cultures in which we
are involved. Our resources are impounded until our people
are awakened from sleepwalking through the American dream of
material achievement, which has become a child-devouring
nightmare for our families. The energies we need to build
the Kingdom are almost wholly absorbed now in hard slavery
to build Mammon and Moloch. We may not need to dismantle
our systems, but we need to die to our old priorities and re-
organize our lives across Christ's Kingdom, in order to gain
the vision and freedom to adapt and reform them. We are not

called to a new legalism of visible poverty, but to a rein-
vestment of our energies in ultimate concerns.

And so, the church must pursue repentance. We must pursue
it until she can preach it naturally and credibly in her evangelism. She must be able to call for comprehensive repentance
from the sins the prophets attacked: idolatry (including unbiblical religious beliefs and systems), personal immorality,
and injustice. Evangelicalism might set a good example for
Eastern and Western Catholicism by repenting of her assumption
that she is the whole of the body of Christ instead of a part
of it with gifts to contribute. And she might do the same
for other Protestants by repenting of her failure to subject
her mind and life fully to the Holy Spirit speaking through
the Word.

Nevertheless, we strongly feel that a part of our *metanoia*
must be a new gratitude to God for the amazing works of grace
He has already accomplished in our midst. While the Spirit,
the world, and the Devil are critiquing the clay in each of
us, we must fix our outward gaze on the diamonds in one another. We must repent of despising one another's immaturity.
Instead of insisting that every brother and sister must have
our gifts and our concerns, we must begin to concentrate on
seeing that the whole body is properly joined together and
fully equipped. We are in the infant stages of renewal. God
has given us a wave of evangelism and surrounded us with spiritually hungry children. He has given us a wave of literature
to feed them; we must wean them from milk to meat. He is giving us a concern for new and renewed institutions to educate
them, and these are being planted; we must see these through
to completion.

He is giving us the concern to resist the moral decay in
our society, a longing to establish justice and mercy, and
prophets to see that we do not forget these burdens. He has
poured out upon us gifts which we hardly know what to do with
as yet: artists and musicians to beautify worship, theologians to reform the church and interpret it to the world, and
many other natural and supernatural gifts. A part of our repentance, and a part of our very mission in the world, is to
awaken fully to these gifts and the Giver in worship and gratitude for one another, and for the wonderful works of God.

II. THE MISSION OF THE CHURCH IN THE CONTEXT OF THE 1980'S

The mission of the church in the next decade remains what
it has always been: to proclaim the Good News of the divine,

crucified, and resurrected Lord to the ends of the earth; and
to make disciples. In the 1980's we can no longer tolerate
warfare between Christians who are concerned to proclaim the
Word for the conversion of individuals and those concerned to
demonstrate it through works of social healing. We must urge
both to find a biblical theology with a place for one another
and begin to work in harmony.

In the 1980's we must have a new vision of the unreached
world which focuses on subcultures as well as tribes and nations. If they and we are divided from one another by lin-
guistic, cultural, or political walls, we must pray and work
and study until the walls are down and the Gospel goes through.

In the 1980's we can no longer entrust the mission of the
church to professional clergy whose main function eventually
becomes a chaplaincy devoted to keeping the laity marginally
alive in the American rat race. The laity must become a mission team to build the Kingdom of God through their vocations,
and the clergy must relinquish their delusions of omnicompe-
tence and move into those limited enabling functions for which
their gifts equip them. If this pattern can be modeled in
America, it can be modeled anywhere.

III. SPECIFIC STRATEGIES OF RENEWAL AND MISSION IN THE 1980'S

Reformation, spiritual renewal, and mission are related to
one another as the body, breath, words, and deeds of a human
being. We cannot expect to aim at one of these in isolation
and achieve the goal of mission.

We have not fixed with much certainty on specific strategies through which these goals may be achieved in the 1980's.
We refer the reader to Dr. Winter's paper, and anticipate
with thanks his continued fertility in ideas, and the fruits
of study and prayer issuing from the Center of World Mission.
New strategies for the local congregation in home missions are
constantly being evolved, lived out, and described as the Holy
Spirit leads us.

We are convinced, however, that the first essential strategy for missionary proclamation and demonstration is *prayer*.
We know from Christ's words and from experience that only
prayer to the Lord of the harvest can produce laborers enough
to reap it. As Jacques Ellul tells us, this is the only force
capable of moving the mountains involved in social change. We
cannot understand the mind of Christ and even comprehend what
mission means from moment to moment in our situation apart

from sharing His mind through intercession. And prayer is essential for the comprehensive reviving and empowering of the church by the Holy Spirit which is essential to mission. Here are some matters we might begin to pray about:

-- We should build into the individual and corporate prayer life of every congregation a detailed intercessory coverage of every nation and subculture on earth, praying for the planting, spiritual renewal and sustenance, and extension of the church in all places. This intercession should be nurtured and armed by up-to-date, accurate information.

-- We should pray for the reviving, reformation, and extension of the church in America, an important base for world missions. We should ask for the purification of the Evangelical Movement, and for its openness to valid criticism and instruction from the rest of the church. We should pray also for the increasing penetration of evangelical values in the large denominations and other sectors where the name of Christ is named. We should pray that the minds of the leadership of American Christianity will be made captive to biblical truth. We should pray for real spiritual and theological unity.

-- We should pray toward the increasingly effective use of media -- especially television, films, concerts, and other expressions of art -- for evangelistic purposes. Pray for Christian television which is so excellent and so skilled in reaching non-Christians that it forces a raising of the standards and values of the industry.

-- Pray for the establishment of new Christian schools on every level, and the raising up of Christian scholars to reinvigorate existing universities and seminaries.

-- Pray for a unified Christian counterattack upon cultural decay, especially the causes and effects of the sexual revolution, teenage pregnancies and abortion, drug usage, and other evils which in this century we have grown to expect and tolerate rather than to resist and conquer.

-- Pray for a similar unified attack upon key social
   evils in this country, and in every place touched
   by American business, government, and missions.
   Begin to pray aggressively about peace and nuclear
   threat, the world economic situation, hunger, environmental reform, political structures, and issues
   of justice. Especially pray for a congregational
   vision of Christian social responsibility, focused
   on needs in the local community and in nearby
   metropolitan areas.

Study of issues vital to home and foreign missions is a
second essential strategy. This study should relate the
whole counsel of God in Scripture to existing situations at
home and abroad. Theological and apologetic responses to
new and threatening trends in the 1980's should be started
and carried through by evangelicals, and not merely corrected when nonevangelicals have done them wrong. Evangelicals in a renewed church should aim at a position in which
they again become the cutting edge of cultural renewal, in-
itiating positive change instead of merely reacting to decay
or to inadequate responses.

Preaching at home and abroad should focus on biblical exposition applied directly and powerfully to current needs.
It should be based on an understanding of Scriptural teaching on Christian experience and spiritual growth, and it
should challenge congregations to initial conversion and to
continued sanctification and empowering by the Holy Spirit.
Preaching and teaching should aim at producing congregations
of persons whose ultimate vocational priority is the building of the Kingdom of God, who are delivered from unrecog-
nized captivity to the American race for survival and success.
The whole church and its members should seek to adopt the
lowest economic lifestyle adequate for ministry and mission,
thus strengthening their witness and releasing funds for the
extension of the Kingdom. Increasingly, laypersons should
be equipped with an understanding of theology, apologetics,
and church history, as well as a comprehensive knowledge
of Scripture.

All congregations should seek for a renewal of the experience of corporate worship. All vital churches in an area
should meet together for encouragement and mutual edification,
and their leaders should join in prayer and strategy for the
extension and deepening of the Gospel witness. Large churches
should carefully test their real impact for the Kingdom, along
with numerical growth, and should foster the subdivision of

the congregation into small groups for prayer, nurture, pastoral ministry, and mission. All local concern and activity should continuously be planned and evaluated against the background of a vital involvement in foreign mission, so that the goal of world missionary expansion is never lost sight of while the renewal on the home front necessary for that expansion is eagerly pursued.

Scenario: Study Group #3

Ted Ward

NEWSLETTER OF THE SMYRNA FELLOWSHIP OF ALBANY

This week is special for all of us in the Smyrna Fellowship. Just five years ago our period of preparation began.
Now that 1984 is only two weeks away we give thanks for the
faithfulness of our God. Some of the things that have happened to us have been unexpected; many things have been difficult. Our people have become more beautiful through service. We have been tested, but God has kept us faithful.
The period of preparation has been worth all the effort.

We remember with thanksgiving the beautiful lives of
Florence and Ed Wilson. They were faithful even to death;
they have received the crown of life. Now our sister church
in Richmond, where the Wilsons were ministering during the
emergency, has been renewed and has taken on the management
of the city-wide reconstruction project. We have been promised four of their people, Bob and Dorothy Devoe and their
son Jonathan, along with Donald Jensen, a carpenter. They
will be joining Millie and Art Baldwin and the Chavez family
in the apartments over the Dearborn Avenue Community Center.
With their help, the Baldwins hope to establish an expanded
ministry of reconciliation in that multi-racial neighborhood.
Pray for them.

How thankful we are that God led us to establish our
"Agenda of Contrasts" in 1980. Ever since, we've been keenly
aware of the ways that being God's people makes a difference

in our values and lifestyle. And we've learned the value of working together.

The two experimental housing projects are reporting more and more visitors. Somebody out there is watching! The Simplified Lifestyle units in the Kroger Block are all occupied now, and most of the residents are active in the fellowship that meets in the Kroger Center. Three of these families are new Christians and are engaged in their family development and discipleship studies with the Rodriguez and Davis families.

Charlotte Allen and Dottie McGuire report a low balance in the Deacons' Fund. Their work on the south side among the Richmond refugees has been more costly than expected. Much of the expense has been for the refurbishing of the clinic and job-placement center. (A special thank you to the two physicians from Pleasant Ridge who have helped our brother, Dr. Steve, taking turns supervising the clinic.) Please consider this a special call for the Deacons' Fund. By the way, for over two years now the fund has been in the black. The simplified lifestyle studies we began in 1979 have paid big dividends. "Abundant grace has been upon us all." We can truly say today that "There is not a needy person among us."

On the subject of funds, the outreach station in Sumatra has sent a special request. Our missionaries there, the Murdoch family, report that their newest church has asked that we consider sharing the costs of a village evangelization campaign. The Indonesians plan to send two of their own people out and our help is needed for two motorbikes. This will be on the agenda for our monthly business meeting next Tuesday. (We hope that Pastor Mike and representatives of the outpost church in North Albany can get in for the meeting although the busses aren't running.)

For almost a year we have managed to hold to our pledge to each other in the Parent-at-Home campaign. According to the last three quarterly fellowship surveys, none of our under-sixteen children are now being left alone at home. The importance of father's or mother's presence in the home has cost several families some income, but apparently they feel the price is worth paying. Many thanks to the voluntary aunts and uncles who are helping out. If rumor has it right, some of the singles involved in this campaign since 1982 have gotten more out of it than the children!

The Richmond experience was a grim reminder that the hand of God is all that stands between us and catastrophe. Forces

far beyond us are threatening. Only our Lord keeps us cool.
The world news surely looks bad. The oil embargo is likely
just the easy part of the bad news. Be especially alert for
signs of deep anxiety among your non-Christian friends. In
Christ we have the only message of comfort and encouragement
that makes any sense at all. Let your compassion reach out
in love.

The next disaster relief training workshop will be held
in January. Those who have not renewed their Relief Speci-
alist certificates since 1982 should try to get updated. A
letter from the mayor's office commends our fellowship, along
with several other groups of believers. It's good that Christians can be counted on in times of need. We live in strange
times. Many are frustrated, others are complacent, and in
one way or another most people outside of Christ seem to have
given up hope. Of course, the fact that this is the forty-
third day without electricity doesn't help one's spirit much.
(You can see by the typing here that we're back to the old
Royal. Pastor Fred sold the IBM Selectric the day before
the power went out. We got $200 for a white elephant. Fred
isn't feeling very moral about it.)

On the bright side -- maybe there will be more Christians
ready to give up television and automobiles now that they've
discovered how to do without. God works in mysterious ways
His wonders to perform!

On the energy matter, Charlie Hill is managing our woodlot
now. Extra hands on the saws are needed this weekend. We've
been supplying wood to several families in need on Division
Street. There's plenty of wood, but Charlie needs help.

If you ever get discouraged, sit down with one of our
children and discover how much they are learning and how creative they really are. The combination of simpler lifestyle
and emphasis on inventiveness that Wilson Mathews and the
teachers in our human development center have built into the
new program is having a clear-cut effect. Our children are
surely a source of renewal and encouragement for our community. We are being asked almost every day by non-Christian
parents if we can open the center for their children. This,
too, we will discuss in Tuesday's meeting. It's not an easy
question to answer.

The key message is the resurrection. The Lord is risen!
In a few days it will be Christmas. What better time to talk
to your neighbors about Jesus. Suggestion: Since lots of

folks face a rather strained holiday season, spread some joy. What about a Christmas party for the children in your building or in your block?

Maybe a Christmas tea for your neighbors. Keep the whole picture of Christ clear: God loved. Christ came. He died that we might have life. He lives! We, too, share His new life.

If there's one thing we've learned in the five years of preparation, it is that God made us all different. Remember how often we clashed in the first two years. It was all lock step. We assumed God wanted all of us to hop in unison. What sense of liberty came to our fellowship the night Stan preached about Zaccheus: "Jesus pulled him out of the tree, went home to share his experiences and resources, gave him a whole new life, but didn't make him one inch taller."

Maybe that's the way we ought to look at the sharp conflict we have experienced over our political action committee. Those of you who feel strongly about this, just do what you need to do decently and in order, respecting the convictions of the saints. Take your stand, make your speeches and petitions, and show the city that Christians care. Surely we should keep a biblical spotlight on the relationship between legislation, societal systems, and injustice.

Keep all of us informed, but don't twist any arms. Some of our brothers and sisters aren't comfortable when you make our church a fulcrum for political leverage. They won't hold you back; in fact, in various ways each of us will support you. Seek the mind of Christ.

Take a look at your new calendar. Should the Lord tarry, the New Year will bring that fateful number, 1984. In the strength of the Holy Spirit of God, may we rejoice in sorrow, make many rich through our poverty, having nothing, but possessing all things. 1984? It's another year to use for God! Peace. Revelation 2:8-11.

Scenario: Study Group #4
Ralph D. Winter

Members of our group gave more time to getting to know each other than to working out detailed, final conclusions. Out of many sheets of earlier observations, we have chosen to present a selection of three "slices" or representative characteristics we anticipate for 1984; then in each case we have suggested appropriate mission goals to deal with those characteristics; thirdly, we noted for each the ways of getting to those goals.

Our first slice was the state of the *family* in 1984. We anticipate a continued breakdown of the two-parent pattern as single-parent households increase to 50 percent. Related to this conditions, our mission goal for 1984 is to see the widespread, organized, deliberate modeling of Christian families to non-Christian families. The way we can reach that goal seems to require the development of a theology of marriage and the family; the development of family-life pastors, family clinics, and outreach by both congregations and special organizations.

Our second slice was to try to anticipate the future concerning the *church as an institution*. We share here just two characteristics we foresee; the continued decline of true worship and the continued decline of accountability within the congregation. Goals we believe essential to meet these needs include, on the one hand, a greatly heightened sense of what worship is, and the widespread development of sub-congregations or what some have called "mini congregations"

within the larger urban churches where accountability seems
to suffer the sharpest decline.

Our final slice was to look at *the world* itself, specifically the world outside the church but *inside the U.S.* Here
we foresee continued fragmentation, moral disintegration,
energy depletion, displacement of urban poor, and the continued trend to morality by consensus.

Goals to meet these needs include the development within
congregations of specialized outreach along the lines of cultural differences, some to reach people like those in the
congregation, others deliberately to develop contact with
people of different cultural, religious, or economic backgrounds. We see the need for Christians to attain key positions in society, and the need for the increase of professional associations of Christians that can more specifically
and extensively define standards of morality from a Christian
perspective within those profesions.

Some of these goals are also means; but we can see the
need to move toward a simple lifestyle, not as individuals
but in groups committed to a cooperative approach both in
buying and in consumption levels. We see the need for everything from a theology of lifestyle to plans for well-
established evangelical families to adopt disadvantaged
families and to work and share together with them over an
extended period of time.

In conclusion, I must record, with some personal pain,
that by the time we finished talking about the family in the
U.S., the church in the U.S., and society in the U.S., we
found we had no opportunity to venture out to the rest of
the world.

Scenario: Study Group #5

Cathy Stonehouse

The most certain word of this conference is that we live in a world of change. Change is in process on all fronts.

VIEW OF THE FUTURE

In the social arena the depersonalization of society will increase. The breakdown of the home will continue. The population explosion in developing nations will provide a growing challenge to missionary efforts.

The church of the future will face decreasing economic resources and loss of tax exemption. Social tensions will increase as the gap widens between the haves and have-nots in all parts of the world, including North America.

Technological advances in the field of communication will provide new opportunities for the church. This technology can be used for evangelism and education.

From the political realm the church will experience restrictions of freedoms. Government regulations will increase sharply in the areas of finance, education, health, and safety standards.

Within the next decade much of Latin America and Africa will be under communist control, and the U.N. will be dominated by communistic representatives. The communist world, however, will be more divided than ever before.

The North American church will probably be operating within a totalitarian regime in the not-too-distant future.

On the religious front we will see the rise of a "Mind Sciences" religion. At first, scientists will be more open to metaphysical answers to problems, but the "Mind Sciences" religion will be anti-Christian.

There will be a lowering of denominational barriers even between Protestants and Catholics, possibly resulting in loss of clarity in doctrine. Christians must also be prepared for the polarization of secular society and an increasingly dedicated group of believers.

Society is on the verge of a transformation. We do not believe that this transformation will take place peacefully. During the next decade the church will exist in a world torn by conflict and increasingly unfriendly to Christianity.

When we compare the conditions of our times, however, with conditions present at the beginning of the great spiritual awakenings in America, there is a glimmer of hope. Conditions are ripe for a moving of God's Spirit and a third great spiritual awakening.

DIRECTION FOR THE FUTURE

To face the challenge of the future, the church must clearly define its purpose and mission. The primary purpose of the church is to bring persons to Christ and lead them to maturity in Christ which prepares them to minister the transforming grace of God in their community.

To do the will of God expressed in the Great Commission, the evangelization of the unreached peoples of the world must be a prime priority of the church and every Christian.

The church must prepare believers in the midst of conflict and suffering to witness for Christ, serve with unselfish love, and stand for righteousness in every aspect of life -- social and personal.

Out of the definition of purpose and mission must grow a clear set of priorities. In the light of present affluence, but the dark view of the future, the church has two priorities: one, to seize immediate opportunities such as:

-- evangelizing the open areas of the world

-- channeling the affluent resources of the West into
   world evangelism and compassionate service

-- challenging youth to involvement in spiritual
   ministries to the world

-- utilizing communication technology for Christian
   education and evangelism

-- awakening and enlisting the church to meet the
   needs of its community.

The second priority is to prepare people for Christian
life and witness in a day of reduced resources, limited freedom, and possible oppression. In relationship to these priorities, ministry to the family must in reality become a top
priority for the church.

Evangelicals in North America have been deeply influenced
by the values of their society. The church must develop a
clear understanding of biblical values and use it to continually and conscientiously criticize values and societal
structures. Part of the preparation both for world evangelization and Christian living in an unfriendly culture is the
identification of values based on biblical principles and
the differentiation of those values from strictly culture-
bound values.

RESPONSES FOR THE FUTURE

How will the North American church change in response to
the needs of the next decade? The depersonalization in society calls for a more personal ministry. This can best be accomplished by a small church. The chaos of society will create more personal problems and hurts which the church will be
asked to heal. A large church with multiple staff and ministries seems to be needed. Financial crises will make it difficult for medium-size churches to support the needed staff
and ministries. The answer may be a multi-level church.
This church would sponsor small assemblies -- mini-churches
meeting in homes -- to provide the needed personal ministries.
The mini-churches would be part of a regular, larger assembly
where they receive the inspiration of the large group and are
visible to the world. The larger body would support the
needed multiple ministries.

The crisis in the family also calls for structural changes in the church. Schedules must be revised to encourage family togetherness.

New programs are needed which minister to the family. Marriage and family enrichment should be an ongoing part of the church's ministry. Parents need help in making their homes the primary Christian education institution for their children. They also need help in knowing how to resist cultural pressures. Instruction in these areas as well as marriage enrichment could be provided on video cassettes to be used in the home.

The church should be active in preventative counseling. Pastors should be trained in pre-marital and post-marital counseling. The congregation should take responsibility for supporting, during the first crucial years of marriage, couples married in their church.

The church needs to be an extended family in our mobile society of partial families. Churches will need strategies for developing this ministry and making cross-generational experiences meaningful for all involved.

Values and principles must be applied in specific situations. Knowledge is needed to rightly apply the principles. The church should help make knowledge available. This might be done through a "Center of Concerns" which would be a forum to bring together persons with the knowledge of specific situations. International Christians, for example, might be consulted for understanding of military issues in their part of the world. Encouraging world travel while this is still possible will also increase the awareness of Americans to world needs.

In our fellowships we should be modeling the love of Christ. While the local church must be concerned for global needs, it must also respond to opportunities for ministry in its immediate community. Communication links must be established with all Christians in our areas. Through communication we can discover our responsibilities to one another and how best to fulfill those responsibilities.

Christians are called to live as pilgrims in an alien society, acting as ambassadors.

Though the church will seek to be the conscience of society, it will be largely unheeded. Perhaps the most apt

metaphor of the church is the field hospital. Even today it
must more effectively minister the Gospel in the midst of
traumatic social conflicts and impending economic and political ones. Quite possibly the church will be forced into an
underground role. It must then bear uncompromising witness
to Christ at the cost of suffering and death.

Scenario: Study Group #6

Larry W. Poland

THE CHURCH IN A CONVULSING WORLD: A TRIANGULAR PERSPECTIVE

OLD PERSPECTIVE

In this Consultation, as in the daily newspaper, we have again been confronted with the frightening and spectacularly grim realities of our world. While we do not for a moment discount the reality of either nuclear threats or aggressive violence in families, dystopian structures in society or the exhaustion of fossil fuels, Group 6 desires to go on record as possessing a *Christo*pian, *not a dystopian perspective.*

Confronted by the overwhelming challenges of our day, we rejected the hope of some vague "transformation" based on psuedo ethics. We were stirred to the confidence that we saw in Joshua and Caleb in their minority report about the promised land. We are not denying the size of the giants. We are merely comparing them with the size of our God. We are not discounting the magnitude of the impending deluge. We are not even counting on the relative security of the ark. We are looking beyond both to the God of Heaven and His rainbow.

With this perspective as a backdrop, we present a triangular view of the future which highlights the *challenges*, the *responses* evoked by them, and the *opportunities* provided by them. Or, if you will, the deluges, the arks, and the rainbows.

A Triangular View of the Church

We see the *challenges* to the church in North America to be:

1. The increasing impingement of secular values on the
church with the world in the Christian as great a challenge
as the Christian in the world.

2. Increasing financial pressures cutting discretionary
funds available for giving.

3. The subtle mixing of truth and error in pagan society
to the confusion and perversion of believers.

4. Emerging problems of church discipline to maintain
any semblance of purity in a church penetrated by an amoral
pragmatism, a hedonistic super-saturation, and a spectator
mentality fed, in part, by the Christian radio and television
bombardment with its superstar mentality and big business
credibility problems.

In *response* to this, we propose:

-- Inter-church cooperation *at every structural level*
   (local, metropolitan, inter-denominational, inter-
   agency) in *concerted and extraordinary prayer*

-- Continual emphasis on the importance of knowing, obey-
   ing, and proclaiming God's infallible Word and incarnat-
   ing that Word in a holy and utterly distinctive lifestyle

-- A streamlining of church priorities to emphasize the
   "pure functions" of the church, stripping away irrele-
   vant and peripheral programs, expenditures, and pre-
   occupations

-- A systematic identification, development, nourishment,
   and support of emerging godly leadership -- male and
   female -- to raise the standard of Christ above the
   battlefields

-- The training of pastors to equip the laity for the maximum possible multiplication of person-power for the
   challenges of the church and relieving pastors of the
   "one man band" role.

Extending even beyond the anticipated effectiveness of
our responses, we see *opportunities* for *supernatural accomplishment* in the:

-- Unlimited potential for communicating God's good news
   by laser, compute telecommunications, and cheap, mass-
   produced wristwatch-sized television sets tied to
   scores of satellite-bounced broadcast frequencies

-- And in the spiritual void in the lives of millions created by sensate over-saturation, psychological anxiety
   paralysis and ideological disillusionment. We expect
   to fill that void with the resurrection life and power
   of Jesus of Nazareth.

A Triangular View of the Family

The *challenges* to the Christian family of the 1980's we
see including all the distressing dynamics attacking *non*-
Christian families, including the special challenges of teaching and modeling spiritual principles, dealing with increasing numbers of single parents (married and unmarried), and
healing the fragmentation of homes and personalities.

In *response* to these challenges we propose:

1. Making every church and Christian organizational *staff*
living models of the successful Christian home -- homes in
loving order as a prerequisite to continued service.

2. Developing creative counterparts to the extended family by "adopting out" singles to married, youth to the aged,
aged to middle-aged families, and children to singles for
temporary but repeated expressions of love and community.

3. Instructing all believers in the basics of biblical
role models, family priorities, and the rediscovery of spiritually enlightened *self-denial* in the pursuit of agape love
relationships.

We see *supernatural opportunities* in:

-- Tapping the resources of increasing millions of retirees
to be "spiritual grandparents" to the church

-- The unlimited attraction of the love of Christ to those
jaded by eros without agape and scarred by relationships without divine resources

-- The potential of reactivating a kind of Global YPCA --
Young Persons Christian Association to provide fellowship, spiritual instruction, family help, and evangelistic outreach to poor and rich alike -- carnage from
the destructive machinery of pre-anti-Christ, totalitarian systems.

A Triangular View of the Global Mission

We see *challenges* to our Lord's missionary mandate to be
so overwhelming as to tempt us to opt for the leeks and
garlics of the world instead of pressing for the milk and
honey of the Kingdom. Resisting that temptation, we cannot
ignore:

-- A continuing population explosion (barring a nuclear
decimation of population) which will keep pace with
and, at points, eclipse the increase of the Gospel

-- The probability of the 2.7 billion unreached increasing
to 4.5 out of 7 billion population unless a dramatic
improvement in the Great Commission impact is effected
immediately

-- We see the challenge devising (to say nothing of implementing) specific strategies for reaching:

Jews	Village dwellers	Muslim
Arabs	Culturally near	Hindu
Urban dwellers	Culturally distant	Chinese

and complex combinations of the above (culturally distant rural Muslim Arabs).

But believing that our God is greater still than *all these*
challenges, we *respond* by:

-- So permeating the church with a "world Christian" perspective that we create missionaries from the *cradle up*

-- Reallocating resources through a "no frill" redistribution of Christian wealth to focus them on the last
frontiers of the unreached

-- Including a world evangelism *spirit and content* in
every Christian education curriculum *every* year at
every curricular level

-- Establishing and supporting a creative and contemporary
world missions periodical, keeping the challenge of the
unreached before evangelicals everywhere

-- Insisting that every mass meeting of Christians, including Billy Graham and Luis Palau crusades, Campus Crusade
Explos, and Here's Life rallies and other crusades and
media outreaches give *bold challenges* for missions involvement with an *invitation* to respond.

In conclusion, we see *opportunities* of galactic magnitude
in the challenges.

-- We see the opportunity of a rising generation of young
people out to change their world -- and changing it
for *Christ!*

-- We see the *depth in Christ* we will possess when our
faith muscles have been exercised sufficiently to embrace victory over these obstacles.

-- We see the thrill of watching our God bring down the
walls of the "closed countries" only to discover that
millions of Rahabs dwell there with their families in
secret faith.

-- We see the *joy* of watching the Holy Spirit bridge race,
language, culture, age, generation, and self-interest
to fashion a mighty army of saints marching in the "one
accord" of Pentecost to attack the gates of Hell.

-- We see the gates of Hell crumbling and the Lamb that
was slain stepping forward to claim the title deed to
the universe amid the *final proof* that our God was
able -- people of *every* tribe, language, kindred, and
nation standing there *with us* and singing the new song.

But in anticipation of that final PTL we urge a confident
shout of FTL. FOLLOW THE LORD. FOLLOW THE LORD. Because we
see that a God big enough to create the deluge, creative
enough to plan the ark, and faithful enough to hang the rainbow is *also* loving and gracious enough to make us all Noahs
-- if we will just FOLLOW THE LORD. FOLLOW THE LORD until
"He shall reign wher'er the sun doth its successive journeys
run."

Scenario: Study Group #7

David E. Johnston

As our group looked to the future, we felt ourselves incapable of assessing the validity of extrapolating into the
future the trends we see around us today. It is not that we
are doubtful that any particular trend will come to pass, but
it is too dangerous to make specific assumptions, based on
current trends.

This hesitance to extrapolate applies not only to secular
trends, but also to the trends within the local church. An
agenda for "1984 and beyond" deals with the intermediate
future. We do not wish to put particular emphasis on trends
which may be a hundred years in coming to pass. We sense,
however -- and we went about our task with, as one of our
members put it -- a concern for "white water ahead." We are
reminded that at the end of it all, there is utopia in the
return of Christ; but, in the intermediate future, we see
danger.

We are concerned about the potential for social class upheaval due to the inability to satisfy rising levels of expectation, both here at home and in other countries. We
sense that the trend to political totalitarianism may continue and that the threat of secularization in the church
may be strengthened.

The threat of major war concerns us. Nonetheless, since
we are not able to assure ourselves that one or another of
these trends will occur as projected, we do not draw specific conclusions on the basis of individual eventualities.

We conclude, however, that regardless of the outcomes, the concern for the mission of the church must be internalized by its entire priesthood -- all believers -- so that in the eventuality of the coming of the "white water," the church will be able to continue on and carry out its mission. We have an *uncertain future*, but we have a *certain mission*. We do not emphasize particular programmatic strategies; rather, we emphasize the importance of broad *commitment to* and *implementation of* our primary mission.

We had some frustrated preachers in our group who decided we should have three "C's" as "pegs" upon which to hang our comments. These pegs are *C*ommission, *C*ommandment, and *C*ommitment. We had a fourth, but I knew enough to reduce it to three!

Our *commission* as evangelicals tells us what we are to do. It is found in Matthew 28:20. Our commission has two aspects: we must *preach the Gospel*, and we must *teach* observance of Christ's teachings. Our concern for crying social needs is included within this statement of our primary mission: we are not only to preach the Gospel, but we are to teach observance of all things Christ commanded. We have a responsibility to preach a holistic Gospel. As John Perkins (a participant in our group) said in his presentation to us together, we don't want to make the kind of Christians who discriminate on the basis of race or who will become materialistic in the face of poverty.

The *how* of our mission may be found in the *commandment* of Christ that we love God *and* our neighbor. Spreading the Gospel is more than explaining the plan of salvation; it involves more than explanation of doctrine; it involves modeling. The church must *model* the commandment of Christ that we love God and our neighbor. We must become implanted where the church does not exist. This applies to areas of our own society where the church is not functioning as well as throughout the world in the major unchurched areas.

The third "C," *commitment*, is our strategy for carrying out our mission. In Ephesians 2:10, we are told that we have new lives in Christ and that those lives are to be spent in helping others. We must actively involve the laity of the church in caring for the needs of those around them. Programs designed by the church leadership must be carried out by a *committed* laity. Nathan Bailey pointed out to our group that we have a responsibility to pray specifically to the Lord of the harvest that He might bring forth committed workers.

Admittedly, this presentation is simplistic, but then, what five- to seven-minute presentation of a scenario for the future is not?

I started out by listing several negative and pessimistic trends. However, we must not head into the future in a spirit of fear. Neither should we be under constant pressure to re-focus our energies in the face of shifting sands of secular trends. After the Great Commission, Jesus said, "Lo, I am with you always" -- *He* is the Lord of the future!

Mary Crowley brought to our group a constant message of hope and motivation to action. She reminded us that leaders in other days often failed to carry out their responsibilities because of fear. She reminded us of Deborah's response to Barak's inactivity in the face of fear of the future. In Judges 4:14, Deborah, quoting to Barak the word of the Lord, said: *"Up, for this is the day! Hath not the Lord gone out before you?"*

World evangelization must be the number one concern of Christ-
ians and the church today. The worldwide ministry to which
God called Billy Graham many years ago is the impetus of the
Billy Graham Center at Wheaton College. Referring to the
Center, he said:

> Thousands of Christian leaders throughout the world
> sense a great urgency for world evangelism *now*.
> They believe that we must work as never before to
> spread the Gospel throughout the world. This Cen-
> ter is born of that urgency. I pray that the Cen-
> ter will be used of God to prepare dynamic, Bib-
> lical evangelistic leadership, combined with loving
> humanitarian concern, to meet the tremendous
> challenges in the years ahead.

Conceived to meet those challenges, the Center will house
these strategic programs:

1. An archives to collect, preserve, and make available
to researchers materials relating to the history of evangelism and missions, including those of the many ministries
of the Billy Graham Evangelistic Association.

2. As one of the world's most comprehensive collections
of writings on evangelism, missions, and revival, the library
already includes the largest collection on evangelism and revival in the English language.

3. Wheaton College Graduate School, now offering M.A. degrees in Biblical studies, communications, and Christian ministries, will have greatly expanded and equipped facilities for training young men and women to fulfill the Great Commission. Further support is provided by the Center through endowed scholarships for Third World students enrolled in the Graduate School.

4. A museum graphically portraying the evangelical message down through the centuries to the present-day many-faceted ministry of Billy Graham and his associates, will also include a unique history of evangelism in America.

5. Other programs of seminars, conferences, institutes of evangelism, etc., related to furthering the goals and purposes of the Center in its worldwide ministry, such as the sponsorship of the 1977 and 1978 "Consultations on Future Evangelical Concerns."

Strategically located at the crossroads of America, the Center is a division of Wheaton College--with its more-than-a-century history of spiritual integrity--and of which both Mr. and Mrs. Graham are graduates and trustees. It will serve as a major international training and leadership resource for evangelical Christianity.

Books by the
William Carey Library

GENERAL

American Missions in Bicentennial Perspective edited by R. Pierce Beaver, $8.95 paper, 448 pp.

The Birth of Missions in America by Charles L. Chaney, $7.95 paper, 352 pp.

Education of Missionaries' Children: The Neglected Dimension of World Mission by D. Bruce Lockerbie, $1.95 paper, 76 pp.

Evangelicals Face the Future edited by Donald E. Hoke, $6.95 paper, 184 pp.

The Holdeman People: The Church in Christ, Mennonite, 1859-1969 by Clarence Hiebert, $17.95 cloth, 688 pp.

Manual for Accepted Missionary Candidates by Marjorie A. Collins, $4.45 paper, 144 pp.

Manual for Missionaries on Furlough by Marjorie A. Collins, $4.45 paper, 160 pp.

The Ministry of Development in Evangelical Perspective edited by Robert L. Hancock, $4.95 paper, 128 pp.

On the Move with the Master: A Daily Devotional Guide on World Mission by Duain W. Vierow, $4.95 paper, 176 pp.

The Radical Nature of Christianity: Church Growth Eyes Look at the Supernatural Mission of the Christian and the Church by Waldo J. Werning (Mandate Press), $5.85 paper, 224 pp.

Social Action Vs. Evangelism: An Essay on the Contemporary Crisis by William J. Richardson, $1.95x paper, 64 pp.

STRATEGY OF MISSION

Church Growth and Christian Mission edited by Donald McGavran, $4.95x paper, 256 pp.

Church Growth and Group Conversion by Donald McGavran et al., $2.45 paper, 128 pp.

Committed Communities: Fresh Streams for World Missions by Charles J. Mellis, $3.95 paper, 160 pp.

The Conciliar-Evangelical Debate: The Crucial Documents, 1964-1976 edited by Donald McGavran, $8.95 paper, 400 pp.

Crucial Dimensions in World Evangelization edited by Arthur F. Glasser et al., $7.95x paper, 512 pp.

Evangelical Missions Tomorrow edited by Wade T. Coggins and Edwin L. Frizen, Jr., $5.95 paper, 208 pp.

Everything You Need to Know to Grow a Messianic Synagogue by Phillip E. Goble, $2.45 paper, 176 pp.

Here's How: Health Education by Extension by Ronald and Edith Seaton, $3.45 paper, 144 pp.

The Indigenous Church and the Missionary by Melvin L. Hodges, $2.95 paper, 108 pp.

Literacy, Bible Reading, and Church Growth Through the Ages by Morris G. Watkins, $4.95 paper, 240 pp.

A Manual for Church Growth Surveys by Ebbie C. Smith, $3.95
paper, 144 pp.
Mission: A Practical Approach to Church-Sponsored Mission Work
by Daniel C. Hardin, $4.95x paper, 264 pp.
Readings in Third World Missions edited by Marlin L. Nelson,
$6.95x paper, 304 pp.

AREA AND CASE STUDIES

Aspects of Pacific Ethnohistory by Alan R. Tippett, $3.95 paper,
216 pp.
A Century of Growth: The Kachin Baptist Church of Burma by
Herman Tegenfeldt, $9.95 cloth, 540 pp.
*Christian Mission to Muslims - The Record: Anglican and Reformed
Approaches in India and the Near East, 1800-1938* by Lyle L.
Vander Werff, $8.95 paper, 384 pp.
The Church in Africa, 1977 edited by Charles R. Taber, $6.95
paper, 224 pp.
Church Growth in Burundi by Donald Hohensee, $4.95 paper,
160 pp.
Church Growth in Japan by Tetsunao Yamamori, $4.95 paper,
184 pp.
The Church in Africa, 1977 edited by Charles R. Taber, $6.95
paper, 224 pp.
Church Planting in Uganda: A Comparative Study by Gailyn Van
Rheenen, $4.95 paper, 192 pp.
Circle of Harmony: A Case Study in Popular Japanese Buddhism
by Kenneth J. Dale, $4.95 paper, 238 pp.
*The Deep-Sea Canoe: The Story of Third World Missionaries in
the South Pacific* by Alan R. Tippett, $3.45x paper, 144 pp.
Ethnic Realities and the Church: Lessons from India by Donald
A. McGavran, $8.95 paper, 272 pp.
*The Growth Crisis in the American Church: A Presbyterian Case
Study* by Foster H. Shannon, $4.95 paper, 176 pp.
The Growth of Japanese Churches in Brazil by John Mizuki,
$8.95 paper, 240 pp.
The How and Why of Third World Missions: An Asian Case Study
by Marlin L. Nelson, $6.95 paper, 256 pp.
*I Will Build My Church: Ten Case Studies of Church Growth in
Taiwan* edited by Allen J. Swanson, $4.95 paper, 177 pp.
Indonesian Revival: Why Two Million Came to Christ by Avery T.
Willis, Jr., $5.95 paper, 288 pp.
Industrialization: Brazil's Catalyst for Church Growth by C.W.
Gates, $1.95 paper, 96 pp.
The Navajos are Coming to Jesus by Thomas Dolaghan and David
Scates, $4.95 paper, 192 pp.
*New Move Forward in Europe: Growth Patterns of German-Speak-
ing Baptists* by William L. Wagner, $8.95 paper, 368 pp.
People Movements in the Punjab by Frederick and Margaret Stock,
$8.95 paper, 388 pp.
Profile for Victory: New Proposals for Missions in Zambia by Max
Ward Randall, $3.95 cloth, 224 pp.
The Protestant Movement in Bolivia by C. Peter Wagner, $3.95
paper, 264 pp.

Protestants in Modern Spain: The Struggle for Religious Pluralism by Dale G. Vought, $3.45 paper, 168 pp.

The Religious Dimension in Hispanic Los Angeles by Clifton L. Holland, $9.95 paper, 550 pp.

The Role of the Faith Mission: A Brazilian Case Study by Fred Edwards, $3.45 paper, 176 pp.

Solomon Islands Christianity: A Study in Growth and Obstruction by Alan R. Tippett, $5.95x paper, 432 pp.

Taiwan: Mainline Vs. Independent Church Growth by Allen J. Swanson, $3.95 paper, 300 pp.

Tonga Christianity by Stanford Shewmaker, $3.45 paper, 164 pp.

Toward Continuous Mission: Strategizing for the Evangelization of Bolivia by W. Douglas Smith, Jr., $4.95 paper, 208 pp.

Treasure Island: Church Growth Among Taiwan's Urban Minnan Chinese by Robert J. Bolton, $6.95 paper, 416 pp.

Understanding Latin Americans by Eugene Nida, $3.94 paper, 176 pp.

The Unresponsive: Resistant or Neglected? by David C.E. Liao, $5.95 paper, 168 pp.

An Urban Strategy for Africa by Timothy Monsma, $6.95 paper, 192 pp.

Worldview and the Communication of the Gospel: A Nigerian Case Study by Marguerite G. Kraft, $7.95 paper, 240 pp.

A Yankee Reformer in Chile: The Life and Works of David Trumbull by Irven Paul, $3.95 paper, 172 pp.

APPLIED ANTHROPOLOGY

Becoming Bilingual: A Guide to Language Learning by Donald Larson and William Smalley, $5.95x paper, 426 pp.

Christopaganism or Indigenous Christianity? edited by Tetsunao Yamamori and Charles R. Taber, $5.95 paper, 242 pp.

The Church and Cultures: Applied Anthropology for the Religious Worker by Louis J. Luzbetak, $5.95x paper, 448 pp.

Culture and Human Values: Christian Intervention in Anthropological Perspective (writings of Jacob Loewen) edited by William A. Smalley, $5.95x paper, 466 pp.

Customs and Cultures: Anthropology for Christian Missions by Eugene A. Nida, $3.95 paper, 322 pp.

Manual of Articulatory Phonetics by William A. Smalley, $5.95x paper, 522 pp.

Message and Mission: The Communication of the Christian Faith by Eugene A. Nida, $3.95x paper, 254 pp.

Readings in Missionary Anthropology II edited by William A. Smalley, $9.95x paper, 912 pp.

Religion Across Cultures by Eugene A. Nida, $3.95x paper, 128 pp.

Tips on Taping: Language Recording in the Social Sciences by Wayne and Lonna Dickerson, $4.95x paper, 208 pp.

THEOLOGICAL EDUCATION BY EXTENSION

The Extension Movement in Theological Education: A Call to the Renewal of the Ministry by F. Ross Kinsler, $6.95 paper, 304 pp.

The World Directory of Theological Education by Extension by
Wayne C. Weld, $5.95x paper, 416 pp., *1976 Supplement only,*
$1.95x, 64 pp. booklet
Writing for Theological Education by Extension by Lois McKinney,
$1.45x paper, 64 pp.

REFERENCE

*An American Directory of Schools and Colleges Offering Mission-
ary Courses* edited by Glenn Schwartz, $5.95x paper, 266 pp.
*Church Growth Bulletin, Second Consolidated Volume (Sept. 1969-
July 1975)* edited by Donald McGavran, $7.95x paper, 512 pp.
Evangelical Missions Quarterly, Vols. 7-9, $8.95x cloth, 830 pp.
Evangelical Missions Quarterly, Vols. 10-12, $15.95 cloth, 960 pp.
*The Means of World Evangelization: Missiological Education at the
Fuller School of World Mission* edited by Alvin Martin, $9.95
paper, 544 pp.
Protestantism in Latin America: A Bibliographical Guide edited by
John H. Sinclair, $8.95x paper, 448 pp.
Word Study Concordance and New Testament edited by Ralph and
Roberta Winter, $29.95 cloth, 2-volume set.
The World Directory of Mission-Related Educational Institutions
edited by Ted Ward and Raymond Buker,Sr.,$19.95x cloth,906 pp

POPULARIZING MISSION

Defeat of the Bird God by C. Peter Wagner, $4.95 paper, 256 pp.
The Night Cometh: Two Wealthy Evangelicals Face the Nation by
Rebecca J. Winter, $2.95 paper, 96 pp.
The Task Before Us (audiovisual) by the Navigators, $29.95,
137 slides.
The 25 Unbelievable Years: 1945-1969 by Ralph D. Winter, $2.95
paper, 128 pp.
*The Word-Carrying Giant: The Growth of the American Bible
Society* by Creighton Lacy, $5.95 paper, 320 pp.

BOOKLETS

The Grounds for a New Thrust in World Mission by Ralph D. Win-
ter, $.75 booklet, 32 pp.
1980 and That Certain Elite by Ralph D. Winter, $.35x booklet,16 pp
The New Macedonia: A Revolutionary New Era in Missions Begins
(Lausanne paper and address) by Ralph D. Winter, $.75 book-
let, 32 pp.
Penetrating the Last Frontiers by Ralph D. Winter, $1.25 book-
let, 32 pp.
Seeing the Task Graphically by Ralph D. Winter, $.50 booklet, 16 p
The Two Structures of God's Redemptive Mission by Ralph D.
Winter, $.35 booklet, 16 pp.
The World Christian Movement: 1950-1975 by Ralph D. Winter,
$.75 booklet, 32 pp.

HOW TO ORDER

Send orders to William Carey Library, 1705 N. Sierra Bonita
Avenue, Pasadena, California 91104 (USA). Please allow four to
six weeks for delivery in the U.S.